Reunions

True stories of adoptees' meetings with their natural parents

Sarah Iredale

London: The Stationery Office

Applications for reproduction should be made in writing to The Stationery Office,

St. Crispins, Duke Street, Norwich. NR3 1PD

ISBN 0 11 702150 4

Published by The Stationery Office and available from:

The Publications Centre
(mail, telephone and fax orders only)
PO Box 276, London SW8 5DT
General enquiries 0171 873 0011
Telephone orders 0171 873 9090
Fax orders 0171 873 8200

The Stationery Office Bookshops
49 High Holborn, London WC1V 6HB
(counter service and fax orders only)
Fax 0171 831 1326
68–69 Bull Street, Birmingham B4 6AD
0121 236 9696   Fax 0121 236 9699
33 Wine Street, Bristol BS1 2BQ
0117 9264306 Fax 0117 9294515
9–21 Princess Street, Manchester M60 8AS
0161 834 7201 Fax 0161 833 0634
16 Arthur Street, Belfast BT1 4GD
01232 238451 Fax 01232 235401
The Stationery Office Oriel Bookshop
The Friary, Cardiff CF1 4AA
01222 395548 Fax 01222 384347
71 Lothian Road, Edinburgh EH3 9AZ
(counter service only)

Customers in Scotland may
mail, telephone or fax their orders to:
Scottish Publications Sales
South Gyle Crescent, Edinburgh EH12 9EB
0131 479 3141 Fax 0131 479 3142

The Stationery Office's Accredited Agents
(see Yellow Pages)

and through good booksellers

Printed in the United Kingdom for the Stationery Office
J26773 G3397 C20 10170

Contents

Foreword

Ann Sutton, *Director, Scottish Adoption Association, Edinburgh*

This book provides a welcome addition to the growing number of publications which give a personal perspective on the adoptive experience.

The need for adopted people to gain information and access to their birth details is well known. Research into the subject, as well as the experiences of those who work with adopted people wanting to discover their family history, shows the need many have for information, access to their birth details and, in some instances, contact with the birth family. It is these two strands – research and the direct recounting of experiences – that have been the two major influences in shaping both adoption practice and legislation.[1, 2]

This book brings together the experiences of fifteen people who have two things in common. First, they have shared the experience of being adopted, and second, they have all chosen to walk the path to meeting one or both of their birth parents. Their experiences are specific and highly individual, as are their personal histories and the circumstances surrounding their adoptive families. Also, their stories are not yet complete. Indeed, they will never be complete – because 'reunion', like any other relationship, changes with time.

The accounts that follow reveal some common themes. Even though each story is intensely personal and textured, many adopted people experience similar questions and feelings, not only during the reunion process, but through their whole life. Issues such as the importance of the name given to them at birth, a frustrating sense of 'not belonging' and a deep sense of loss even in the presence of a happy and positive adoptive family combine with questions such as, 'Who am I like?' and, 'Why was I given away?' There are also the fantasies – 'What if?', 'What would it have been like?', 'My real parents would have been better', or even 'I was kidnapped.' On top of all this are the problems many adopted people suffer on milestone occasions such as birthdays, mother's day, and sometimes father's day. These questions and themes speak to some of the underlying issues of adoption – loss, attachment and personal identity.

We cannot escape the fact that adoption involves loss for everyone involved: for the adopted child because they cannot live within their birth family, and also, for the birth parents who relinquish their child through the legal system or voluntarily. There is also loss for adoptive parents. Some have to deal with the loss of not being able to build their family through birth, so they therefore choose to adopt. Other adoptive parents may feel 'loss' in the time they missed with their adopted child – the time the child spent in foster care, or in their inability to comfort the child earlier.

While prospective adopters and some birth parents will have opportunities to consider and discuss the implications of their decisions, this process never actually reaches an end. Adoption is a lifelong state, and experiences and losses will continue to be re-worked and affected by subsequent life stages and events.[3]

In the 1940s, '50s and '60s, many adoptive parents were encouraged to see adoption as a new beginning for everyone involved. As will be seen in many of the following accounts, they were encouraged to 'tell' their children about adoption and use the word 'adoption'. They were also encouraged to use the words 'special' and 'chosen' when explaining things to the child. Perhaps it is only now, a few decades on, that we can see that such terms raise difficult issues in themselves. For example, if as an adopted child you were 'chosen' because you were happy, might you not be also 'unchosen' if you were naughty? Furthermore, in order to be chosen, some earlier separation will have had to have occurred and some new attachments therefore made. In David's story (page 140) in particular, we can see how an adopted child might react negatively to this 'chosen' label.

By the 1980s, the emphasis had changed. Adoption workers encouraged adoptive parents to develop a greater understanding of the birth parents, and to assimilate actively the positives from the child's 'first' family experience into the child's life history.

It was the adoptive father and sociologist H. David Kirk who contributed much to this new way of thinking. In his book, *Shared Fate,* he urged much more openness in adoption. Openness between adoptive parent and adopted child would naturally involve openness with the birth parent – in the form of sharing information on an ongoing basis. He was, I think, arguing for a genuine acceptance of all that brings an adoptive family together.[4,5,6]

Of course, this openness can be difficult for adoptive parents. How do they get the story right when they tell their child? How can they tell it without hurting him or her – especially when many children's first family histories are convoluted with pain? The hard truth is that they cannot eradicate the child's hurt, or their own.

Another aspect of adoption which causes difficulty is the use of the word 'real'. 'You are not my real parents', 'My real parents wouldn't make me .... would understand better.' Statements such as these have a familiar ring to adoptive parents and adopted people. What, therefore, is 'real' parenting? What are the qualities we can respectively ascribe to birth and adoptive parents? Do adopters always feel themselves to be 'real' parents? Whatever words we use, adoptive families need to acknowledge their difference in relation to other families, and to be strong in their 'sameness'. This 'acknowledgement of difference'[4,5,6] is a strength when it comes to families addressing their losses and their gains. Adoptive parenting is real, but different: it has extras. The tasks, however, are the same as in all families: to help children develop good, secure attachments and give them a safe base on which to build their personal identity. The differences must not be a barrier to the development of close, loving, family relationships which are necessary to emotional health.

The other issue for adoptive parents is the need to be aware of the adopted child's concerns as they grow up. They need to know their child will 'fantasise' about their other family, interact with that fantasy, and will therefore need real information and facts to slot alongside it. The child's questions and concerns will evolve with age, and will also be inextricably linked with the subject of sex and family-building.[7] The answer is, as always, to exchange information and questions openly: to discuss and talk things over with the child on an ongoing basis.

Yet all this – the talking, discussions, the openness – will never extinguish the desire of many adoptees to meet with their birth family. But because there is more communication between adoptive parents and child – on an honest, understanding and respectful level – the child may feel much less guilt about seeking a reunion, and the parents may well feel less anxious and fearful. There may also be less fantasy, and when, ultimately, the adopted child comes face-to-face with their birth parents, they may well find that the people they meet are much 'closer' to the mental pictures they have held in their imagination.

If we acknowledge that adopted people have experienced loss and separation and other events which have affected them deeply, then how do they heal from these? I hope that for many, the experience of adoption is a substantial contribution to that healing process.

Van Gulden and Barfels-Rabb point out, 'An adopted person can heal without searching or finding, can search and find and still not heal, or can search and find and heal. The overriding objective must be to heal: to grieve the loss, find resolution and come out of it all with a positive sense of self.'[8]

However, the path to that positive outcome will almost certainly be complicated and does not require a 'happy ending'; rather a process which allows the individual to progress through to 'resolution'. This will also often take time, sometimes years.

At a reunion itself, there may be an instant spark of recognition and affinity between the adopted child and the parent. But after that, there are more dilemmas and 'choices'. These revolve around the questions of 'What next?' and 'Where do we go from here?' The use of the word 'choice' is difficult in this context. 'Choice' was limited at the beginning of an adoption, so the options after a reunion are restricted as well, for everyone involved.

Adopted people who have gone through reunions will recognise the 'what next' syndrome, and some of the dilemmas a meeting with a birth parent or parents presents. As well as the problem of different expectations and hopes, and the attitude of other siblings and half-siblings in the birth family, there is also the overwhelming question of 'Who knows?' and the burden that comes with the legacy of secrecy carried through from the time of the adoption itself. Other common themes include a powerful urge to go forward; initial elation, buoyancy and delight; sometimes anger and frustration.

As an adoption worker, I would encourage anyone working towards reunion to take advantage of the opportunities available for talking, discussing, counselling and mediation. This can be provided both by professionals or the growing networks of birth parents and adopted people offering help and support right from the first contact through to the actual meeting and beyond. This kind of support may be especially positive when the search, and the finding, are very rapid. Modern technology such as the Internet is increasingly a factor in 'condensing' the searching process. In Andrew's story (page 45), for instance, computer links meant he was able to trace his natural father in the US within three days.

Like many of my colleagues, I owe much of what I know to what people directly affected by adoption have told me in person – birth parents, adopted people and adoptive parents. I am constantly grateful to them for sharing their experiences and feelings to a level and depth that exposes their rawness and pain, as well as their best hopes, dreams and expectations. It is this knowledge which, when combined with the theorising, can better equip us to help other adopted people and their families.

All of those who read this book will surely be grateful to the fifteen people who have shared their stories thus far. I hope very much that both birth parents and adoptive parents will find the accounts a useful way of 'hearing' their children. I also believe that the stories will have a very real significance for adopted people themselves. The knowledge that others have shared their feelings – or at least some of them – and that these emotions are therefore 'normal', has a very special value. And more so when it comes not from social workers, counsellors or adoptive parents – but from people who are, like them, adopted.

References

1. Triseliotis, J., 'In Search of Origins' (1973), London: Routledge, Kegan & Paul.
2. 1975 Children's Act, Section 26; England & Wales.
3. Rosenberg, E.B., 'The Adoption Life Cycle' (1992), New York: Free Press.
4. Kirk, H. D., 'Shared Fate' (1964), The Free Press. Enlarged edition (1984), Ben-Simon Publications.
5. Kirk, H. D., 'Adoptive Kinship' (1985), Ben-Simon Publications.
6. Kirk, H. D., 'Looking Back, Looking Forward' (1995), Perspective Press.
7. Bernstein, A. C., 'Flight of the Stork' (1994), Indianapolis: Perspective Press.
8. Van Gulden, H. and Barfels-Rabb, L., 'Real Parents, Real Children' (1994), New York: Crossroads.

Preface

Like most people who weren't adopted, the issue of adoption and the experiences of adopted people were largely alien to me before I started to compile this book. I was the ultimate outsider, someone who knew little about the subject and its many implications, not only for adopted people themselves, but for their biological families and adoptive families too.

I was lucky enough to have been brought up by my birth parents and to share my childhood with my natural siblings and extended family. Like others who had the same, I took the emotional and physical security of my upbringing almost totally for granted, unaware of how much my knowledge of my roots contributed to my sense of belonging and stability. It has been a tremendous privilege to learn just how important that 'completeness' is.

Knowing what I know now, I can only admire the bravery of the thousands of adoptees who decide to face up to their past and who risk much in tracing their natural parents. And there are risks. Whatever their adoptive family situation, no adoptee when taking the first steps to trace their natural parents can ever know what is around the corner. As many of the following accounts show, the actual reunion meeting itself is not the end of the process, but only the beginning. From there, it is often a rough and rocky road, where the feelings and futures of many people have to be considered, managed – and possibly – ultimately interwoven. And it is, usually, the adoptee themselves – as the instigator of the reunion – who bears the burden of managing and tempering the repercussions of their actions. If they felt alone before starting out, then their sense of isolation may well be compounded by the need to cope with the emotions of all those affected by their decision.

Happily, many reunions do have positive and fulfilling outcomes. But in putting together this book, I have endeavoured to cover the whole spectrum of experiences. Some adoptees are no longer in touch with their natural parents, some maintain irregular contact, others have built caring and long-term new relationships. But most, whatever the outcome, feel that in some way, just seeing and meeting their blood relatives – even if it is only once – is enough to help complete their sense of personal identity. Most of those whose stories are told in the following pages have had the questions that haunted them through childhood answered.

I owe much to the adopted people who have agreed to share their stories in this book. Not only have they given their time freely, they have opened their lives to me, a complete stranger, in a spirit of great trust. I wish to thank them all for their generosity, honesty and courage in talking about aspects of their lives, many of which they have previously kept hidden from the outside world. I hope very much, as they do, that their experiences will help and inspire other adoptees who read this book whether they pick up the gauntlet of tracing or not.

My sincere thanks also go out to everyone who has assisted me in putting this book together: to Bridget LeGood at The Stationery Office, a very wise mentor; to Ann Sutton, Director of the Scottish Adoption Association, for her kind and enthusiastic support as well as her practical help; and to Judy Smith, whose contacts and research into adoption issues increased my understanding of how it has affected so many lives.

Last but not least, I want to thank Jude, Annie and Sarah for their inimitable support over the last year.

Sarah Iredale   *September 1997*

Hugo

I was adopted when I was ten weeks old by a comfortable, middle-class couple who lived outside Northampton. I was their first child. My adoptive dad was a brewer in the town, while my adoptive mum was thirty-six and unable to have children. Two years after adopting me, they adopted a baby girl to complete the family. Apart from three elderly grandparents, we had very little contact with other relatives. I met the odd second cousin now and then, but that was it.

I always knew I was adopted, although I can't remember being told. I just accepted it as part of me and never wondered about my natural family. It really wasn't an issue for me, Mum and Dad or my sister.

We moved to Surrey and I was packed off to boarding school. At best I coped with the place, but I always looked forward tremendously to going home. But after a few years, the trigger happened.

I was in my last year at school and my mum died. She'd been ill for a year or two, but I had no idea how serious it was until a few days before, when Dad told me she was dying. I was sixteen when it happened, yet I barely grieved. I never cried. Maybe I'd lost touch with her because of my time away, whereas Dad and my sister had dealt with her illness every day. But what I do know is that I was not as unhappy as those around me thought I might be. I had little chance to talk with my sister or Dad, because once the funeral was over, I was back at school.

Even at this stage, I still didn't consider checking out my 'replacement' 'real' mum. The summer afterwards, my sister and I ran our house like a permanent party area – Dad didn't get back from work until eight most evenings, and when he did, he was occasionally fairly drunk: his way of dealing with his grief. I continued to feel that my adoptive mother was my only mum. But, soon, we did get a replacement of sorts.

Almost exactly a year after Mum died, Dad remarried. He married Mum's best friend who had recently been divorced and who was also my godmother. It was an unmitigated disaster. The three of us moved out of the home we loved and into our new mother's rambling farmhouse nestled in the Cotswolds. After a year of screaming, fighting, arguing and crying from just about everyone (she had three daughters we knew as friends), the unhappy couple separated and we moved out.

By the summer of 1982, I was in London re-taking my A levels and all the ingredients from the past couple of years were beginning to have an effect. All it would take was a catalyst of some sort to stir me into action.

Around my eighteenth birthday, my sister showed me some documents concerning both our adoptions. The most interesting ones were the 'adverts' for us. Mine described me very flatteringly – 'almost perfect in every way' – and then gave a brief outline of my birth parents, although mainly my mother. There she was in six lines – age, features, interests, the fact she was a teacher, and, most intriguingly for me, that both she and my father were Canadians.

Dad found out that we'd seen the letters and just shrugged his shoulders. But I still didn't do anything for four or five years, apart from occasionally fantasising about potential meetings with my mother in places like Waterloo Station. I think it was still just intrigue that eventually forced me to consider tracing her. I knew from the documents that she had had me alone, and I wasn't bothered about seeking my natural father.

It was two years later that I got things moving. Once started, it took on a huge momentum. Once I'd got my records and my original birth certificate from St Catherine's House, I was put in touch with a social worker. She warned me of the pitfalls – the obvious possibility of rejection and the fact that my mother could well be back in Canada and therefore be nearly impossible to trace. She could even be dead. I then went back to St Catherine's House and my social worker said she'd delve further into my records.

I did pretty well. I already had my birth mother's full name, and this time, I discovered she'd got married in England and had two children. The last was registered in 1969. Thereafter, there was no trace of the family. Extremely chuffed with my detective work, I went to see my social worker the next week. She'd done better than me. She'd found my mother.

Apparently, my birth mother, who was living in Canada, had written to a friend in England who had been a neighbour of hers, asking her to release information about her if anyone ever came looking. My social worker had contacted the friend and had also got hold of a photo of my mother – Beverley – which she handed to me. I looked at the photo and was immediately struck by the resemblances. (When I later showed it to a friend, they remarked that it looked like me with a wig on!) I was then told that a letter was already winging its way to Beverley telling her the good news.

I have to admit that I was very hung-over that particular morning. I remember being annoyed with myself that my headache wouldn't go away enough to take it all in. Later though, I started to feel better and just kept staring at Beverley's photo, thinking, 'That's my mum, that's my mum!' I was looking at a blood relative for the first time.

Until this point, I had had lots of friends to talk to about what was happening and hadn't felt the need to tell my adoptive family. But now I felt I ought to tell my sister, although I was a little wary of her reaction. After all, I had found a 'new' mother and she hadn't. She was fine about it though, and very happy for me. She did tell me though that she had also done some groundwork into finding her natural mother, but that things had ground to a halt. She had also told Dad about her hunt. He had not been happy and had mumbled something about questioning her love for 'Mummy'. Knowing this, I decided to wait and see how my reunion with Beverley went before telling him. If it went well, then I would tell him; if it went badly, then no-one need ever know. A bit of cop-out maybe, but I had made my decision and I felt a great weight lift from my shoulders.

My first contact with Beverley was by letter. Me to her first and then she wrote back. It all happened extremely quickly. Within four weeks of my meeting with my social worker, there was a letter on the doormat from my natural mother. I left it there while I made some breakfast. After half an hour or so, I picked it up, sat down with a cup of coffee and opened it. In it, she said she'd received my letter and described it as a 'wonderful shock'. She told me more about the family. Her son and daughter (my half-brother and half-sister!) were two and four years younger than me and neither knew of my existence. The only family members who knew were her mother and her husband. To make matters more complicated, she had recently separated from her husband – amicably – the man she'd married in England.

She then went on to tell me why she had given me up. It was something that had never concerned me: I hadn't traced her to give her a hard time about that. She had been a young, single mother in a foreign land in the mid-1960s and things had been very different then – a cliché, but true.

At one point in the letter, she said she could still picture me in the blue outfit she had bought me when was I born, as if it was just a few hours ago. I was extremely moved. My sympathies weren't with myself for what might have been, but with this poor woman pressured by what was expected of her, by what was the norm, into giving up a baby her heart did not want to. She finished by saying she was longing to see and talk to me. The letter was signed 'Beverley, Your Mother'. If I'd been a little anxious about finding her before, I knew now that I'd done the right thing.

During the tracing process, I had been in the middle of preparing a trip to Australia. I now decided to buy a round-the-world ticket, going back via Toronto in Canada to meet Beverley. We had both decided it was best not to meet immediately, so I would stay in Australia for a year or so and then go on to Canada.

The night before I flew, I spoke to Beverley for the first time on the phone. She sounded younger than she was, and still does. We spoke for about half an hour – I can't remember what about – and it was very relaxed and enjoyable. She later told me the phone call was wonderful and that I seemed very familiar to her.

I lived in Sydney from 1989 to August 1990. During that time, I regularly exchanged letters with Beverley, swapped photos and occasionally spoke on the 'phone. Every now and then, I yearned to be in Canada sooner, but I was having such a great time, the longing wasn't as powerful as it could have been. When August came around, I travelled to stay with a friend in Michigan and, after a few days, got on the train to Toronto. By this time, my brother Robert and sister Kathryn had been told about me. Their combined reaction had been something along the lines of, 'Oh ... so he'll be coming here will he? Okay.'

I remember arriving in Toronto vividly, my memory helped by a written journal which I kept at the time. The journey took seven hours and towards the end, thinking I was still half an hour from the station, I grabbed a quick nap. I woke to find that I was, in fact, only five minutes from the station and that I wasn't prepared. In just a few minutes, I would be meeting my mother for the first time. I dived into the toilet to splash water on my face and to check that the spot on my forehead was behaving itself. Luckily, it was. The train stopped and I walked down to the exit point, peering over the exit barrier all the time.

There were quite a few people around, but I had no trouble spotting the figure to the back of the crowd, leaning against a wall. She recognised me as soon as I saw her and gave a little smile. I gave a similar 'un-over-the-top' smile back and went over. I can't remember what we said, but we had a good hug, then a good look at each other, then the same again. My brain was totally fuddled. Beverley then took my bag and walked to the car. As we went along, I tried to be the most likeable and agreeable person in the world. She was more of a talker than I'd expected, and I thought at the time she was a little less good-humoured than I thought she'd be – a false impression as it turned out.

We decided to drive down to the harbour front for a meal. It was a good, clear evening and we sat outside, looking out over the islands in the Metro area and talking about how I'd traced her; about my brother Robert and my adoptive dad. I was as tense as hell, though I'm not sure I showed it. I remember smiling all the time and developing a slight, nervous laugh which I used after any funny, or even unfunny, remark she made.

From there, we drove back to her house, which she'd only moved into a couple of days before. We hugged again before I went to bed. 'Thanks for coming,' she said, to which I replied something stupid like, 'Thanks for having me!' The next morning, she woke me by ruffling my hair which I thought was nice. She went off to work and I introduced myself to Toronto by sauntering around the city. I was due to meet Robert and Kathryn the same evening, both of whom were back at the house when I returned.

Beverley greeted me with another hug and then introduced me. Robert seemed very pleasant. He was also a bit of a talker, although an interesting one, with a good, quick, dry wit. I kept looking at him to spot any similarities, but there was nothing too obvious. Kathryn, who wasn't very well at the time, came downstairs and I immediately noticed more resemblances: something about the eyebrows, the forehead? She turned out to be very mellow and nice.

I then met Beverley's mum, who was seventy-eight at the time, and Chris, her ex-husband, Robert and Kathryn's father. We then all went to a Japanese restaurant for dinner. The meal was good, but everything was fairly quiet what with Kathryn being ill and some tension between Chris and Beverley. I felt myself getting more and more tense and could hardly hold my chopsticks together as I was shaking so much.

Once we got back home, it all started to sink in. Here I was, surrounded by four blood relatives. Two days before, I'd never met any blood relatives. I felt ready to crack up if I didn't do something, even if it was just to cry. For some reason, I couldn't cry, so before I went to bed, I gave Beverley an extra big hug. I put my head on her shoulder and told her how everything was sinking in and how nervous I'd been all day. She told me that her mother had been close to breaking point too. I said that I was pretty close to breaking down in some form or another. Beverley replied that I should let it happen. I was trying to let it all go, but I guess I must have still been too tense. Anyway, another hug and I went to bed feeling a lot lighter. I suppose I was feeling that I hadn't shown Beverley enough affection until then, and had wanted her to know that I was as happy with things as she was.

I ended up staying in Canada for two months. It was too long. Beverley was back at work for most of the time and although I was happy occupying myself during the day, she obviously felt a responsibility to ensure I was having a good time. She suggested a few times that I might like to travel around the Province for a while – it would have given both of us some much-needed space – but for some reason, I didn't go. I didn't want to say that I was leaving earlier than intended, in case it was taken the wrong way. Despite the problems my long stay might have caused, my abiding memory is how everyone, from my family to my mother's friends, seemed to take the whole thing in their stride. They made me feel as welcome as possible.

I had had no idea that my grandma had been close to breaking point that first evening: she had seemed the most relaxed person there. But a couple of days before I was due to leave, she took me out to lunch and gave me a small, silver-plated brooch in the shape of a maple leaf that had belonged to her husband. It was a gesture that meant a great deal to me.

She didn't make any fuss about it, she just said, 'Here, I'd like you to have this – it belonged to your grandfather.' It was good to have a grandma again.

Robert's and Kathryn's reaction to me was, on the outside, very calm and accepting. Robert had to cope with the concept that he was no longer the eldest child, and we spent a fair amount of time together and got on well. However, we never discussed the fact we were brothers and got on as friends, which was fine by me. We almost touched on deeper things once, after a few drinks, but soon diverted back to how the Toronto Blue Jays, the city's baseball team, were doing. He also kept his activities with me separate from those with his friends and I sometimes wondered whether I was ever going to be invited to one of his games of roller-hockey. I never was. I guess he needed a break from it all.

I didn't see much of Kathryn during my time there. I stayed with her for a few days in Peterborough where she was studying, and although we got on fine, I found myself trying too hard again and didn't relax. She seemed much more relaxed than me and that didn't help matters.

Since 1990, both Robert and Kathryn have come over to England independently, but it wasn't until my next trip to Toronto in 1995, that I got to know them better. I stayed for two weeks and by this time, both of them were living in the city, so it was easier for the three of us to meet up. They seem a very close brother and sister, but I never once felt unwelcome. I've now discovered we have quite a lot in common – musical and reading tastes, political views, and a generally laid-back demeanour. That's the one thing that has been apparent since I've met my Canadian family – we've never had to force ourselves to look for an affinity. I get on with them all naturally, as people.

One event in 1995 stands out. Robert, Kathryn and I went out on the town one night with a couple of their friends, and Robert introduced me as 'My brother Hugo'. It was the first time I'd been referred to in that way.

The fact that I haven't met the family that often over the last six years because of the distances involved has been frustrating, but I also think it has been an advantage. The first over-long meeting excepted, there has been little chance of over-exposure and my relationship with my Canadian family has stayed fresh. Second, this way there is far less threat to my adoptive dad. If my natural family had lived in England, he might have found the whole affair more difficult to accept.

The hardest part of the whole experience was telling Dad about my visits to Canada. He knew I'd been there, but had thought I was staying with friends. About a year after my first visit, I plucked up the courage to tell him – with the help of several pints of beer in the local pub. I told him I'd done a bit of tracing for my birth mother, and he didn't make much of a response.

'In fact,' I finally managed to say, 'I've found her and visited her in Canada.'

There was hardly a flicker from him, although he just managed to nod his head. He then said something like, 'If that's what you want, then that's fine.' The burden that lifted off my shoulders was so great, I wouldn't have been surprised if a two-ton grand piano had floated up to the ceiling.

After that, Dad took the whole thing extremely calmly. He's never once spoken of his feelings about the subject – he's not someone who does – but he has shown his acceptance of Beverley in other ways. Once I'd told her that I'd told him, she wrote to him thanking him for raising me. They've now met on three occasions.

When it comes to the future, I haven't made any definite plans. If I wanted a Canadian passport I could get one, but at the moment I have no desire to leave England. I think that as long as my dad is alive, I won't go abroad. He is very much my father and I feel I should be in the same country for his remaining years. If he should die, it might well be a watershed moment in making my decision as to where I should live in the future.

One thing I do know is that the whole course of events seems to have happened very naturally. Nothing had to be pushed. Beverley feels very much like my mother. If I'd felt that I was forcing this relationship, any relationship, to work, then I would have known it wasn't working. Thankfully, this never happened.

Janine

If you believe in fate my friend,
Then take a look at me ...
Do you think this is really how my life is supposed to be?

Janine, 1996

Adopted? Yes, I am. I've always known, but I've always carried the scar of adoption. And like any scar, it's opened many times – every time a play or drama on the subject comes on TV, every time I read an article in the papers about it, even when family relationships are discussed, salt is always poured into the wound. That, I suppose, is the one thing you learn to live with: the scar of adoption.

Despite my reticence to face the subject, I had always been aware of the inexplicable bond between me and my birth mother. I had often thought about her, worried about her, hoped she was well and happy. I knew, always, that she loved me. And in difficult times, I had turned to her in my mind for comfort, for support, for a guiding light. In her, I had trust, I had belief. She was my religion.

I suppose, like any other adopted person, I used to walk along the street looking at other people, wondering if I was related, studying their faces thinking: 'Are those my eyes?' It's such a strange feeling knowing there's somebody out there who is part of you. And all the time, your personality is such a mystery. It's not just the 'Who do I look like?' syndrome, but more significantly, the personality traits which are such an unknown. Sure, you've been moulded by your adoptive family and friends, but you know there's a deeper, ingrained persona which is set in stone. Whose sense of humour, whose temper, whose passions have I inherited? My painful lack of brothers and sisters also left a huge void in my soul.

My being adopted was a cruelty I could never justify, a pain I could never heal. To many, it might have seemed an inevitability, but to me, it was nothing short of deprivation. Who were the people who had decided my future? Who were they to choose my life? What kind of society drove me away? I was an innocent child, and so too, was my mother. Who were they to judge me now?

This individual determination, so vulnerable,
Perhaps my reticence from an era unknown.
A certain touch of class, tainted by the ineptitude of my abilities,
Yet sinfully decent in the spice of life,
Enjoying the comfort of variety.
Echoes …. spiralling round the desire for knowledge, for understanding, for IDENTITY.

Janine, 1990

I was brought up as an only child (the one thing I never felt comfortable with) in a typical, Scottish, middle-class family where pride was utmost and taboo subjects were certainly never discussed. So I learnt to put my adoption to the back of my mind and get on with my life.

At last, however, the time came to do something about it: to confront the issues and release my locked-up emotions. What triggered me off? I don't really know. Independence, my own house, a new job, a move south; perhaps all these things combined to create a certain happiness. I think the fact that I was content and more stable in my life meant that I was finally able to confront what had been hidden away for all those years. I had never known that one day I'd do something about it. To be honest, it had never really crossed my mind. But one day, completely out of the blue, I found myself telling my story to a new friend who knew nothing of my background. After years of keeping the secret, all these ingredients seemed to form the catalyst for what seemed such a natural thing to do: to search for my birth mother, my real family, my roots. Looking back, I had no concept of the magnitude of what I was about to embark on, but I knew I was scared. Until now, society had dictated my life, and now it was my turn. I've always been aware of being fiercely independent – as if I was rebelling against my adoptive parents – loving as they were. It was almost as if I had to cling on to my individuality as the very last trace of my real identity.

The decision to search was easy, in stark contrast to the many subsequent decisions I had to face. A visit to the Citizens' Advice Bureau gave me the addresses and 'phone numbers of the relevant authorities to contact. A few letters soon led me to the Scottish Adoption Association who confirmed that they did, indeed, hold my records.

Nothing could have prepared me for the information that followed: not even a stiff Scotch or three! Details from my personal file and my original birth certificate told me the town I was born in, the time of my birth, my father's age, occupation and hobbies, and – most shattering of all – my mother's name and my original name. Shock, euphoria, confusion: the whole spectrum of emotions engulfed me. For the first time in my life, I found myself in a situation where I didn't instinctively know how to react or feel. Up till then, instinct has been such a natural strength, but now I was being faced with the one thing I hadn't had all my life and I didn't know what to do, what to think, what to feel. I suppose years of suppression hadn't prepared me for it. I felt like a child again.

The Scottish Adoption Association continued to send regular letters revealing more information. They also provided me with compassionate and experienced advice which I would never have sought, but which I found invaluable. Once I had extracted all the information the Association had about me, it was down to me to make the next move. If I was going to pursue things further, I had to visit the Scottish Records Office in Edinburgh to bring my story up to date. I had reached a crossroads. More searching meant no turning back.

My trip to the computerised records office in Edinburgh was exhilarating and, the search, once there, remarkably easy. Bumbling through in Inspector Clouseau mode, shaking with nerves and adrenaline; I found that my mother had married, that I had two sisters, and that, thankfully, no deaths were recorded. A quick search of the 'phone book revealed the family's address and 'phone number. It was all too easy. At last, I had what I wanted. I held the trump card and I was on top of the world!

I didn't know if she was dead or alive.
I stood on the precipice of hell.
And when, at last, I knew she was alive,
I fell back on to solid ground.

Janine, 1994

My search was complete. That momentous day, I'd discovered more identity than I'd ever had before. The anticipation, fear and hesitation had turned to pure excitement and total elation. I had begun to understand myself, to know myself.

The agonies of the next stage seemed never-ending. Now I had to contact my mother. I was so aware of all the information I had at my fingertips. I had her name, address, 'phone number and so many family details. I was very conscious of the power of my situation, yet she knew nothing, and had known nothing for twenty-eight years. Only I could make the next move and it suddenly struck me how cruel this was. I spent sleepless nights considering the effects and implications for her and her family, particularly on her other two daughters – my sisters – who may not even have known of my existence.

I decided to contact her through a letter sent from the Adoption Association. Perhaps the shock would be lessened that way. One wrong move now and I could lose everything all over again. For the first time in my life, my heart was exposed and my fear of rejection overpowering.

The letter was sent and I waited with baited breath. The 'phone call came back the very next day. She had contacted the Association and had been very cool, very calm. 'That's my mother!' I thought. I was so proud of her.

Eight months of agonising followed when she didn't make any further contact with me or the Association. Her 'phone number was etched on my mind, but I was determined that I wasn't going to call her. Was it to be rejection once again? No. Finally, via a 'phone call to the Association, she conceded to a meeting.

Ae fond kiss and then we sever,
Ae fareweel and then forever,
Deep in the heart-wrung tears I'll pledge thee,
Warring sighs and groans I'll wage thee
But to see her was to love her,
Love but her and love forever,
Had we never loved sae kindly
Had we never loved sae blindly,
Never met – or never parted,
Had we ne'er been broken-hearted,
Ae fond kiss – now bring us together ...

Robert Burns

It was a warm Scottish breeze that blew on 2 July 1995, the day of our meeting. Two hours to go and I felt very alone ... poignant, since what was about to happen could end the loneliness I'd lived with all my life. I was expecting nothing and hoping for anything. I'd always gone into this anticipating the worst – rejection – so anything else would be a bonus, right? In a couple of hours, I'd know. My mind was in shock, trying desperately to focus on the enormity of what I was about to do. Hard as I tried, I just couldn't put it all into perspective. My mind was completely numb.

I was staring into the wind, overlooking the Clyde, my heart filled with fear. Fear that my own mother might not like me – how bizarre that sounds! Fear that we wouldn't know each other, that we may not be able to strike the chord which had been severed so long ago. Instinctively, I turned around to see her and her husband walking calmly towards me. I kissed her cheek, she brushed mine. I hugged her and she pulled away as I pushed a posy of flowers towards her. I stared, perhaps too intensely, into her eyes, as she silently fought back the tears, her hands shaking. I felt remarkably calm.

'... and you had a happy childhood?' she launched into conversation.

She took me quite by surprise. My cool demeanour evaporated and my eyes watered. We carried on with some small talk as we walked back inside the hotel where we'd arranged to meet. I grabbed the opportunity to study her more closely – her jewellery, her clothes, a stylish, well co-ordinated woman; her fine hair, her smile, her eyes ... those eyes ... struck a chord deep down, almost as if I recognised them.

I could drown in your eyes,
I could swim in your smile,
Perhaps count the ways that we can reconcile
The years that we've lost,
The time that's slipped by,
The feelings, the touch, the love and the lies.

Janine, 1995

We sat, on edge, in the hotel lounge and I knocked back a large whisky (at 11 am!). I was searching all the time for physical similarities – the hair, the complexion, the eyes ... those eyes ... and personality. As the day went on, we hit on many personality traits and countless behaviour patterns that were the same. The same too, for my two sisters: my sisters who had decided not to come to the meeting. I was deeply hurt by their absence and perhaps showed it. The rejection had come, after all, not from my mother – but from my siblings.

We continued to chat, catching up on twenty-eight years, with her husband freely joining in. He was a generous, gentle man with a sense of humour that was easy to love. I asked my mother how she felt. Her eyes red, her hands shaking, she didn't hesitate.

'Very nervous, very anxious, stomach churning. And in need of another drink!' she replied. I loved her honesty.

'But you look very calm,' she said.

'Oh, I don't feel it. I'm very good at hiding my feelings.' We seemed to have an easy rapport that I'd never experienced before. It was almost as if we'd never been parted.

I was quietly impressed with the ease with which she knocked back the whiskies. Her mind was far away as she relived, in graphic detail, my birth and my adoption. Tears rolled silently down my cheeks as her eyes narrowed with pain and she controlled herself with the resilience of experience.

'I remember Christmas Day,' she continued. 'You were nine days old. I was in a ward with about twenty beds. They'd relaxed the rules that day. Everyone could have as many visitors as they liked and everyone else was surrounded. I had no one. You started to cry and you wouldn't stop. You were in a cot by my bed, but I wasn't allowed to touch you or hold you, except at feed times. Even then, I held you and tried not to let myself love you, but that was hard ...'

Now it all seemed to fall into place: her rather distant approach towards me, the way she couldn't really look me in the eyes, the way she pulled away from me when I first tried to hug her. She had distanced herself from me all those years ago and she was doing the same again now. I realised then that this woman was touching a part of me which had been locked away for so long and I suddenly felt emotions I didn't recognise as my eyes once more welled up with tears.

'They took you away for tests the next day,' she continued, 'and I never saw you again ...'

I was dumb struck. I was overwhelmed by her honesty and sheer composure. We sat back, exhausted, pondering the cruelty of it all.

The next six hours flew by with photographs, family stories, comparisons, observations, questions and answers. It was all very tiring and when at last she left me, she turned to me and said:

'Now I'll go home and think of all the things I should have said to you!'

I thought to myself, 'Oh no, you've said everything – just by coming here today, you've said it all.' I stood and watched the car lights fade into the distance.

It struck me then that I may never see her again, that she'd left me for the second time in my life. I felt very alone and as my eyes grew heavy, I fell into a deep, deep sleep once more, like a child.

'And my soul spread wide its wings,
Flying across the silent land,
As it flew towards home ...'

Janine, 1983

It has now been over a year and we haven't seen each other since. The only contact from her was a telephone call and a card on my twenty-ninth birthday. That must have been so hard for her. It was a very touching gesture which meant the world to me.

Since then, I've been determined to keep the contact going. After all, it would be so easy to lose it all now. My 'phone calls to her have always been very well received (if expensive!). We get on so well; our senses of humour and our personalities seemingly in tandem. But still my sisters won't accept me. We haven't met and we haven't spoken. That hurts me so much. Perhaps I place too much importance on that, but I can't help it. They mean so much to me, yet all the time I'm very sensitive to their feelings.

The counsellor at the Scottish Adoption Association has continued to offer me advice and comfort, and throughout everything, has been a great support. Without her, I could never have gone through with the search or the reunion and kept my sanity! I owe her so much.

Now, I feel my life has almost come full circle. I feel a much more complete personality. I have more identity than I've ever had before. I know my mother is slowly coming to terms with the reunion, with the 'umbilical whiplash'. I'll give her time, but not too much time. After all, life is too short, and we have a great future ahead of us – together.

To other adoptees or birth mothers out there, I'd say one thing: '*Carpe diem* – seize the day!'

Fiona

I was born in Canterbury in 1970. My parents weren't married and my father, Nigel, was nineteen and my mother, Wendy, eighteen. He was serving in Northern Ireland in the army. When Wendy and I were discharged from hospital, I was fostered out to a family for a short time.

Nigel and Wendy married when I was about six months old and took me back to Northern Ireland with them. I remember quite a lot from that part of my life: I was left alone for much of the time and later found out that Wendy was having affairs with other soldiers. I've spoken to my father Nigel since and I told him how scared I am of the dark and of fireworks – I hate Bonfire Night – and he said it was probably a memory of all the noise and troubles in the province during the 1970s.

We were sent back from Northern Ireland and from then on, I was passed between Nigel and Wendy, foster parents and my now adoptive parents. At one point, Nigel and Wendy took me back to Northern Ireland without the permission of social workers. Nigel just turned up at my adoptive parents' home – who were fostering me at the time – and said he was taking me. There was nothing Mum and Dad could do.

I was eventually officially adopted in 1972, when I was two years old. Over the next few years, my adoptive mum and dad worked as emergency foster parents for children that were at risk, so there were other children coming and going all the time. They fostered a little girl called Samantha who was with us until she was about three. She was three years younger than me, but we were like twins and did everything together. Even though we weren't related, it was like having a double. Mum and Dad had to give her up because they were regarded as too old to adopt another child, but I remember her vividly. I would dearly love to meet her again.

I don't remember Mum and Dad telling me I was adopted, although they must have done at some stage. I first began to understand it when I started to get hassle at school. The other kids used to tease me by saying my mum and dad were so old they must be my grandparents. I definitely developed a chip on my shoulder about the whole business. Mum never hid anything from me, so right from my early teens I knew in general terms where my birth mother lived. But at the time, I was so wrapped up in my own life – I was starting to have problems at school – that I actually hardly gave it a second thought. Then, when I was fourteen, something triggered everything off. My best friend's mother was a bus driver and over the course of a few months, she became friendly with Wendy, my birth mother. Wendy told her she had had a daughter adopted by an older couple in a particular village, and my friend's mum, Denise, put two and two together and deduced that it was me.

Soon after that, Denise invited me over to her house and told me she'd spoken to Wendy. Straight away, I said that I wanted to meet her. This surprised me as I really hadn't given the idea of a meeting – or the implications of it – much thought. Denise said that if Wendy agreed, we could meet at her house.

I then wrote to Wendy asking her to meet me. There wasn't much to the letter – I didn't want to go into anything too much at that stage. It was just an invitation really. She wrote back, giving her letter to Denise who passed it on to me. I was thrilled when I got it. I had been convinced she didn't want anything to do with me and was finding it hard to accept that she had given me up and yet now wanted to see me.

We arranged to meet on a Saturday afternoon a couple of months later. I'd told Mum and Dad what I was planning to do and had asked Mum if she would go with me to Denise's house on the day. She was fine and agreed. Dad was more diffident about the whole thing and made it clear he was terribly worried that I would get hurt.

On the day itself, I was so nervous I almost didn't go. There was a fairground in town that weekend and after going on a long walk to get my thoughts straight, I went there. I don't know why. I just walked and walked around in a sort of daze. I guess I was just scared and frozen into inaction. Everyone came out looking for me – Mum, Denise, my best friend and her boyfriend. After a few hours, they found me, still wandering aimlessly around. Then they gently took me to Denise's house.

I didn't have to wait long for Wendy to turn up. She knocked on the front door and I stayed in the kitchen while she went into the sitting room. When I walked in, I looked at her and felt nothing. Nothing. The only thought I had was that maybe she did, now, want to know me. Maybe she wouldn't push me away again as she had done in the past.

The two of us sat there for a couple of hours, just talking. We covered everything that had happened during my childhood and she told me most of what had gone on in her life. The only really striking thing was that we were so similar in colouring. Brown eyes, dark hair, olive-coloured skin – it was all there. I was really struck by the physical likenesses, but emotionally, I didn't feel there was any rapport at all.

As the meeting went on, things started to feel really strained. It was as if she was putting on an act. She had hugged me once at the beginning but that was the only time. There was no other physical contact or touching. Looking back, it all seems very strange and I remember the atmosphere becoming quite awkward. In the end, I got up to go and we agreed to meet up again. But I got a strong feeling that she didn't really want to. It wasn't anything she said, she just seemed really cold about it.

We met up again in Ashford, where she lived, about two weeks later. I went to her home and her boyfriend was there, whom I didn't trust. We talked again for a quite a while and she told me about her mother, my natural grandmother, who had lived in Ireland but who had recently died. Wendy told me that her last wish had been to see me walking up her garden path. Hearing that made me feel very emotional.

Wendy and I then went to visit her brother, who lived very near. Even there I felt like an outsider, especially with his wife. Their children were there, my cousins, but that didn't help. It just made me feel more strongly that I didn't belong. We left after about half an hour, which I was pleased about. After that, I went back home, with Wendy saying she would 'phone me.

Mum and Dad knew everything that was happening at this stage. I knew Mum wasn't keen on my seeing Wendy regularly and Dad was even more worried about things. He was still insisting that I'd end up getting hurt all over again.

I carried on meeting Wendy regularly for a couple of months and eventually plucked up the courage to ask her about my real father. She hadn't mentioned him at all and I wanted to know more about him. I believed that just as I had had a right to meet her, so I had the same right to meet him. She surprised me by reacting very well and gave me his address and 'phone number in London straight away. However, she warned me that if I 'phoned him, I should be wary about meeting him. Naturally, I asked why. She didn't give me a straight answer. All she said was that if I did meet him, he'd hurt me as he had done before. I couldn't let that piece of information lie, so I pressurised her to tell me more. She told me that when I had been very young, Nigel had thrown a knife at me and that it had hit her by mistake. I asked her to show me the scar, which she did. She pulled up her jumper and showed me a mark on her stomach. My first instinct was that the scar was the result of an appendix operation – not a knife wound. I didn't say anything. I had a strong feeling she was lying to me.

I went back home that night knowing I had to 'phone Nigel. Having met Wendy, I had a huge urge to see him and know what he was like. I 'phoned him that same night. I was trembling with nerves.

When he picked up the 'phone, he was totally shocked. I thought he was going to die.

'Do you know who this is?' I said.

'Yes I do,' he replied, without any hesitation. He then said he had been wondering when I would 'phone. He told me he'd always known I would contact him one day, but didn't think it would happen so soon because I was still so young. After all, I was still only fifteen.

Once he'd got over the initial surprise, we fell into a conversation and chatted about what he was doing and what he did for a living. I asked him whether we could meet. He seemed delighted. We agreed to meet in Canterbury, just before my sixteenth birthday.

I told Mum and Dad about my plans to meet him. This time, Dad was completely different. He said that as I'd met one parent, I had a right to meet both and that was OK with him. But now it was Mum's turn to react badly. It was like their roles had been reversed. She was very unsure about Nigel and said she would come with me to the meeting. So everything was set up. Mum, Nigel and I would meet in the buffet at Canterbury station on 5 December 1986. I'll never, ever forget it for as long as I live.

We went by bus. Again, I felt incredibly nervous, perhaps even more so than I had with Wendy. I think it was because Nigel and I had got on so well on the 'phone. I really felt there was an unshakeable family bond between us. I felt instinctively that he cared about me. It was all so different from Wendy.

As we walked up to the station, I could see a man sitting at a table by the buffet window. I instantly knew it was him, without any doubt whatsoever. I was terribly excited and as we went in, he immediately stood up. He had known it was me within seconds. It was a wonderful, wonderful feeling.

From that moment on, we talked constantly. The atmosphere was so easy that Mum left after just one cup of tea. She obviously knew things were fine. Nigel and I continued chattering, very naturally, as if we'd been friends for years. We then went into town, had lunch and then – I still can't believe this – went to the local cinema.

I can't remember for the life of me what film was on. I don't think Nigel can either. We just didn't pay any attention to it at all. There were four other people in the cinema that afternoon and they were really annoyed because we just talked all the way through. We had such a good time, it was unbelievable. Everything was really comfortable. We talked about our lives and our plans for the future. It turned out he was a bodyguard for an Arab in London, but he said that he dreamt of starting up his own business. Afterwards, I asked him to come back to meet Mum and Dad. He gently said he'd rather not, as it was too soon for things like that. He was probably right, but I was just so excited.

After that day, Nigel continued to 'phone me every night and we'd chat endlessly. We arranged to meet a second time, again at Canterbury station, a couple of weeks later. Everything was marvellous.

On the day we'd arranged, I got to the station a little ahead of time, feeling really upbeat and happy. I waited and waited. Slowly it dawned on me that he wasn't going to turn up. I sat there for a full five hours. I couldn't bear to think he had let me down. I 'phoned Mum several times, but he hadn't 'phoned. I 'phoned his pager, but there was no answer. I even got some British Rail staff to 'phone British Rail in London to find out about train delays, but everything was running on time. I was in a terrible state. Eventually however, I decided there was nothing else to do but go home.

Just as I got in, Mum told me Nigel had 'phoned only minutes before. Apparently, the batteries on his pager had been flat, so he had been completely uncontactable. I was very upset still. I got straight on the 'phone to him and explained how I thought that he didn't care. He was very apologetic and said that he'd tried calling but had kept missing me.

He came down a couple of days later to meet me after school. He looked so smart – he was wearing a three-piece suit and smoking expensive cigarettes – and I felt so proud he was my father. He came home with me that day and met Mum and Dad. I'd been really worried about how Dad would deal with the meeting, but it turned out very well. Nigel and he sat down, started chatting and got on like a house on fire. They talked about horse-riding, football – every subject under the sun – and I just sat, watched and listened. It was going so well that Dad got out the dreaded family photo album and showed Nigel all the photos of me as a toddler.

My birthday was a couple a weeks later, and Nigel offered to take me out to lunch in London to celebrate. I was desperate to go, but I asked Mum to go with me as I'd never gone to London on my own. She agreed, and we both met Nigel at Charing Cross. Mum then went to visit friends and Nigel and I went on our very own tour of London.

Well, it wasn't really a tour. We were both talking so much that we walked up and down Oxford Street about seven times. We went to lunch at a lovely restaurant in Soho. It was on that day that I began to realise that I truly loved him. It was in such contrast to what I felt about Wendy. While Nigel had taken me out for my birthday, she hadn't even sent me a card. During the lunch, he presented me with a huge birthday card with the words 'To a Very Special Daughter' splashed all over it. I was overjoyed, but when I took it home, I kept it in my bedroom rather than the sitting room so as not to hurt Mum and Dad.

I found out from Nigel that he'd had another child, a little boy, a few years before. He'd since left the mother and was still in touch with Ben, the boy, who was a toddler by this stage. I've never met Ben but am now seriously thinking that I'd like to trace him. He is my half-brother after all.

By this time, it was early spring 1987, and it was then that Nigel dropped the bombshell. He told me he was going back to South Africa where he'd spent some time as a child and that he would be staying there permanently. I was so upset, I shocked even myself. All the old feelings of rejection came flooding back. To say I didn't want him to go was a huge understatement. I just thought, 'Here we go again – he's walking out on me.' That was when the first feelings of bitterness started.

As a recompense for him going, he invited me to the Ideal Home Exhibition at Earl's Court where he was working for the week. He paid my fare up to London every day, so I turned up every day. I was so excited that I decided to dye my hair in celebration, and I went completely over the top. I dyed it blue, gold, pink and green!

When he first saw it, Nigel reacted with horror. He made me go and wash it out there and then – luckily it wasn't permanent. He could be very strict like that sometimes.

A funny incident happened while we were there though. Nigel, his mother-in-law – who was also there that day – and I were sitting in the restaurant when a child at a nearby table burst a balloon. Nigel, because of his job I suppose, just suddenly pulled out a gun. When he realised it was only a balloon bursting, he quickly put the gun away again; but I was shocked and shaken. I knew he was there as a bodyguard and had a licence to carry the gun, but seeing it in the cold light of day was something else. It took me a while to calm down.

He was due to fly from Heathrow on 19 April and invited me to meet him for lunch at the airport. Again, Mum came to the airport with me and then left Nigel and me alone together. Over lunch, I was extremely tearful and emotional. I told him I didn't want him to go and would do anything to make him stay. But there was no way he would or could. Just before he left, he told me not to get pregnant – he knew I was going out with a boy at the time and, of course, I was still only sixteen. Then he left. I was distraught.

What do you think happened? A few weeks later, I telephoned him in South Africa and told him the news. I was pregnant with my first child, James. He hit the roof.

I haven't seen Nigel since, for over nine years. If I can though, I call him around once a month, but mostly, he calls me three times a year: at Christmas, on my birthday and on New Year's Eve. But deep down, I suppose I know that if things were really bad for me and I needed help, he would be on the end of a 'phone for me.

Six years ago, he got remarried; to a South African nurse called Lorraine who has a little girl – Meg – by another relationship. I've spoken to Lorraine a few times and she's sent me postcards when they've all been on holiday. They even sent me a video of their wedding. We get on quite well, but I'm dreading the day we meet. I suppose it might stir up feelings of jealousy on my part. After all, Lorraine has had Nigel for a whole six years: I've never had that. I find myself resenting Meg also. She sounds a great child, but I feel she's had everything that I've missed out on.

I keep trying to persuade them to send me air tickets, but Nigel always says he can't afford it. He's also starting a new job in Saudi Arabia very soon, but it's only a temporary contract, so Lorraine and Meg are staying in South Africa while he's away. I've told him that before he goes to the Middle East, I want to visit South Africa for 5 December this year, as it will be the tenth anniversary of our first meeting. He said maybe.

There's so much I want to say to him. When he first went, I wrote to him so many times asking him why he didn't keep me and if he had loved me why he hadn't hung on to me whatever happened. I was asking all the big questions which I hadn't before. He always said I was too young to understand.

But the last time I wrote to him I said I was old enough to know and had a right to know. I want to know more of the truth. My need to know is fuelled by the fact that Wendy tried to turn me against him. I'm determined to know why she did.

I haven't seen Wendy for two years now. I used to go over every two weeks to see her, but we hit problems when she got over-protective towards my second child, Samantha. She wouldn't let me do anything and was always criticising the way I was bringing her up. She obviously saw both James and Samantha as her grandchildren and I had a problem with that. At one point I told her that I didn't consider them her grandchildren as she had given up that right twenty years before when she'd had me adopted. Mum told me off for saying that. She said 'They're the only grandchildren she's got.' But I couldn't, and still can't, see it like that.

Things came to a head when Samantha was diagnosed as an epileptic and I discovered that Wendy suffered from the same thing. I was very angry that she hadn't told me. But I decided not to confront her. Instead, after everything else that had happened, I just decided it was best to let it all go.

I don't speak to her at all now. She doesn't contact me and I don't envisage anything happening between us in the future. I don't want anything to happen.

It's different with Nigel. I want him to come back, but I don't suppose he will. He's forty-three now and all he has are photos of my kids. He's never met them. I get very annoyed with him now, because I feel that if he'd wanted too, he could have done a lot more for me than he actually did. I don't know anymore how much he really cares for me.

Looking back, I suppose I regret contacting Wendy. From the age of fourteen when I first met her, I went downhill. Before that, I had been really easy-going. I didn't have a temper, and Mum and Dad could have a conversation with me. I was doing OK. But my reunion changed me. I suppose it's because that after we met up again, I began to feel that Wendy was rejecting me all over again.

Now I work on the basis that everyone who has ever said they loved me has left me – Wendy and Nigel to start off with, then my adoptive sister, Samantha; and now Wendy and Nigel again. The only people who have stuck by me are Mum and Dad. I'm so grateful to them.

Susannah

I've known I was adopted for as long as I can remember. I must have been around four or five when my adoptive parents told me, but because I'm half-African, half-English I would have guessed anyway because my parents were white and I had different-coloured skin! Nothing was ever hidden from me or my adopted brother, who was also of mixed race. My adoptive parents also had three natural children, all older than me, who are white, so that was an obvious reminder that I was different.

Because I am of a different race, it's difficult to quantify how being adopted affected me: the two things are very much intertwined. I've always had a feeling of not quite fitting in anywhere and that could be for either reason. At school however, it was definitely my skin colour that made me the subject of mockery – not the fact I was adopted.

All in all though, I had a very happy childhood. I know that I felt insecure, which is a problem I still have. It stems from trying to grasp the fact that I had a mother who didn't want me, or couldn't keep me, when I was a baby. But I've always regarded my adoptive mum and dad as my 'real' ones: even though there may have been times during arguments when I held myself back from saying 'You can't talk to me like that because you're not my real mum' and things like that. Mum and Dad have always treated me and my brother exactly the same as their other children, perhaps even better. I think my older siblings believe we two younger ones have been a bit spoilt!

I started thinking about my birth parents around the age of twelve or thirteen. I know that by the time I was fifteen, I was keeping a diary and my mood swings were like a rollercoaster. I was something of a rebel and would have arguments with my parents that kept triggering things off. I'd think, 'I must find my real mother because she'll give me unconditional love'. There was also a big age gap between me and Mum and Dad – a forty-year gap – and that exacerbated things and made me feel even more insecure. Things built up and I remember that in my late teens, my thoughts were geared towards getting to eighteen and starting to find out a bit more about myself and my natural family.

One particular day, when Mum and Dad were out, I started being nosy. I came across a box of family documents and found some adoption papers relating to me and my brother. On discovering our real names, I thought mine – Wendy Bigg – was horrible. I've got something of a weight problem and it really was the type of name people like me would want to avoid.

When I got to eighteen, I told Mum and Dad what I was planning. I'd made up my mind I wasn't going to do anything behind their backs, so I kept them informed every step of the way from then on. I was also aware of playing down my enthusiasm and excitement about it all. I sat them down countless times and explained I was tracing my birth mother not because of any failing on their part, but because I was curious to know who I looked like and who I could have been. It was traumatic telling them, because I was still very young and badly needed both of them to be around. I knew I had to do it on my own, but I desperately wanted their help. At the same time, I knew it was a little unfair to ask them to support me through my search.

By this time, I knew my date and place of birth, so I went to St Catherine's House and contacted the Social Services. My first trip to St Catherine's turned up my birth certificate and adoption papers, which gave me my birth mother's name – Karen – oddly enough, the same name as my adoptive mother. The space for my natural father had been left blank. My social worker went through my records and we uncovered sketchy details about the situation my mother had been in when she gave me up. I found out that I had an older, full sister. There were a few things about my mother that I found difficult to deal with: she was what was known as 'educationally subnormal'. This was through no fault of her own: her own mother had died when she was three years old and she and her brother and sister were all put into care. She ended up in a special school, where they concentrated on domestic subjects such as home economics. She simply didn't get a proper education.

Other trips to St Catherine's turned up the fact that I had three other half-siblings – another sister, and a further sister and brother by my mother's marriage in 1979. I had a big family out there – and there was also my older, full sister as well! Luckily, my brother's birth certificate gave me a recent address. Although it dated back thirteen years, it was a start!

I telephoned the town hall in the relevant area and asked them to check the electoral register. They rang me back really quickly with good news – Karen was still at the same address. The adrenaline rush I had was incredible. The Social Services then wrote to her saying they'd had contact with someone in her past who wanted to get in touch.

After the letter was sent, I was on absolute tenterhooks. I can't describe the feeling: sheer anticipation, pure excitement and worry all rolled into one. But I never had any doubts. It was something I had to do, even though I knew there was a strong chance she'd reject me again.

The Social Services called me a couple of days later to say Karen had been in contact and wanted to see me. It was an absolutely incredible feeling. I was flying. Apparently, she had known immediately who was trying to contact her and had been delighted. I was very worried about how her husband would react, as he might not have known about me. But apparently, her husband did know about me and was looking forward to a meeting.

I wrote a very long letter back to her, telling her all about me and how I'd grown up, what grades I'd got in school and everything I thought she'd want to know about me. It was difficult to write – where do you start after eighteen missing years? She wrote back immediately and I remember being really touched by the PS on her letter. She said that she'd always remembered my birthday, 26 April, every year. It really meant a lot to know she'd been thinking of me on that day, as I had been thinking of her on the same date.

We exchanged a couple more letters and she sent photos. I never really had an image of her in my mind before, but when I saw her picture, I was surprised. I had obviously had expectations about what she looked like, and she was nothing like them at all. She was a very big lady and I remember thinking 'Oh no!' I scanned the photo trying to find some similarity, but I couldn't see any. It was very strange.

I then rang her. I remember feeling incredibly nervous: after all, this was the woman who had given birth to me and it would be the first time we'd ever have spoken. When she answered, I just said, 'Hello, this is Susannah,' and we started chatting straight away. We got on well and she was very bubbly and lively. I also spoke to my half-sister, Paula, who was only sixteen at the time. She was very shy, but nice. They kept saying, 'When are we going to see you, when are you coming up?' We arranged to meet. We planned to meet at Victoria Station by the telephone booths.

That morning, I was more than just nervous, I was trembling. I remember being on the train – I was by myself – and thinking that I desperately wanted and needed Mum to be there. Every time the train pulled into a station, I was ready to jump off there and then and forget it all. But I knew I couldn't do that. I spent the rest of the time just staring at my watch, wondering whether Karen was going to turn up, what she would be wearing, and whether she'd look different from her photos. It was all amazingly nerve-racking. I was totally on edge.

When I got to the station, I walked up the platform, looking at every face that went by, thinking, 'Is that her, is that her?' I'd done the same thing on previous trips to London while I'd been tracing her: walking down the streets, thinking, 'That could be her, she could be passing me now, she could be just across the road and I'll never know.' It was precisely the same feeling, but now it was fired with this huge anticipation.

I got to the 'phone booths and no-one was there. I 'phoned Mum to tell her I'd arrived and for reassurance that everything was going to be OK. As I put the 'phone down, I turned round to see Karen. I recognised her instantly from her photos. She just said, 'Hello'. We didn't hug. I didn't feel anything really emotional or any instant bond at all. We'd already established a sort of vague friendship on the 'phone, and I felt like I was on a blind date. It was a tiny bit awkward.

We got on a bus to Hackney, where she lived, and during the journey I asked her all the questions I'd always yearned to ask. We hadn't really touched on them before. Who was my father? What had happened? Why had she given me up? Why had I been called Wendy? How much had she thought about me over the years?

She replied that she had an affair with my father, but that he wouldn't leave his live-in girlfriend. She had become pregnant and, without a job or anyone to support her, had simply decided she couldn't cope with me. Her father had also told her that she wasn't welcome back home unless she 'got rid' of me. I was pleased she was being so open about the past.

I started to feel more comfortable with her and although it was still very strange, I felt we were beginning to build a friendship. She suggested we went for something to eat and that I meet her husband, Paul, and my half-brother and half-sister, Stephen and Claudia. We went to a McDonald's and, an hour or so later, all three of them walked in. Paul is black and the two children, like me, are of mixed race. I suddenly warmed to them all – for the first time, I had a feeling of belonging. These were the first blood relatives I'd ever met in my life and the kids were very sweet. Stephen was eight, Claudia about fourteen and both were very shy and accepting. Stephen really took to me and although he probably didn't grasp that I was his older sister, he kept saying I was and sitting on my lap. It was lovely. Paul seemed very pleased to meet me and was careful to stay in the background. His job was to keep the kids under control while Karen and I talked and that's what he did.

Afterwards, we all went back to their flat. It wasn't what I expected: it was in a very rundown, graffiti-covered, North London estate. It was quite awful. We sat in the lounge and Karen got out all the family photo albums. We chatted for the rest of the day. She filled me in on the rest of her life and I told her everything about my childhood and parents.

Paul then drove me back to Victoria Station with the children. There were loads of thanks, goodbyes and plans for me to go back up and meet the rest of the family. It was quite emotional. I got on the train in a complete daze. There were a thousand and one things buzzing through my brain and I was glad I had some time to get them sorted before I saw Mum and Dad again. I couldn't believe that after eighteen years of wondering what my natural mother looked like, I'd at last found out. Now I knew what she looked like and I felt very satisfied with everything. I had no major doubts; I'd got on well with them all.

Dad met me at the station and asked me how it went. I responded that it had gone well. I was very careful not to say too much and not to say too little either. I told him how the day went, concentrating more on the negatives than on the positives, because I didn't want to hurt his or Mum's feelings.

Over the next few days and weeks, I gradually realised that I was happy with where I stood. I had found what I had been looking for. It wasn't a case of my wanting to stop contact – I wanted to keep in touch with my new-found family – but I didn't want things to get more close or intense. As far as I was concerned, I had a mum already and Karen could never step into her shoes.

However, almost immediately after the meeting, Karen started to write and 'phone regularly. I'd hear from her every few days. She started to send me cards with 'To a Special Daughter' on the front – she still does send me those – and I began to feel a little claustrophobic. It was becoming clear we wanted different things from our reunion and it began to become a headache. I began to ask myself how I could explain things to her, and effectively say, 'Thanks, but no thanks'. But I decided I couldn't be so upfront.

In the end, I decided that I would, slowly but surely, back off a little. So instead of answering every letter Karen wrote, I started to answer one out of every two. I was trying to just slow things down a little. I never said anything direct to her about how I felt, but I'd always made it clear to her from the beginning how strongly I felt about Mum and Dad. I thought it was less cruel to back off quietly than actually tell her that I wanted, and needed, my own space.

I knew by then that I didn't love Karen. I cared and sympathised for her, but my childhood dreams of her arriving in my life and whisking me off into another world were no longer there. They'd gradually disappeared over the years and had finally been put to rest by our first meeting.

While all this was going on, I arranged to meet my half-sister, Paula, in London to see how we got on. We made plans to spend the day going around town. Over lunch, she told me all about her life and about how she had been fostered, but had always had contact with Karen. She'd also managed to get some qualifications and get to college – just like me. I felt a powerful bond with her as the day went on. We had our photos taken in a passport booth and we both searched the photos for similarities. It was a lovely, warm feeling I hadn't experienced before. It was great to know that she didn't want anything from me. All she wanted was for me to be myself. It was different – purer – from my relationship with Karen.

Around the same time, my full sister, Samantha, also contacted and met up with Karen. She, like me, had also been adopted after living with my father when she was a toddler. I spoke to her on the 'phone a few times and when I met Karen for the second time, it was arranged that Samantha would be there. By this time, she and Karen had built up a very strong relationship: both had voids in their life that needed to be filled and had found the answer in each other. I think this was because whilst I had found a wonderful adoptive family, Samantha had been passed from pillar to post and had never really had anyone to fill the missing mother role.

When I met Samantha, I recognised her immediately. We look very alike. Although she was bigger than me – she's around twenty stone! – the similarities were obvious. She was very, very bubbly and chatty, and we got on amazingly well. After an hour or two together, I really felt like I had an older sister, even though I didn't know her very well at that stage.

It saddens me that she's had such a difficult life. We are full sisters, but simply by the toss of a coin, she'd ended up with my father who had sexually abused her. In contrast, I'd ended up in a five-bedroom house in the country, with a swimming pool and with a lovely, loving family. I could easily have been her and I think she's been very messed up by it all.

Despite all the bad things I've heard about my father, I'd like to meet him just the once. From what I've heard, I don't think I'll like him. Samantha told me he was originally from Sierra Leone and is a prince out there, but that the civil war in the country means he now has to live in London. But I'm still desperate to find out who I look like and I suppose I look like him more than Karen. I want to meet him one day and leave it at that.

In terms of where things stand now, I can honestly say they're quite good. My relationship with Paula, my half-sister, is great. I've never had any pressure from her. We call each other once every couple of months and it's very easy-going. I also have a good relationship with Samantha. She really is like an older sister, and I go to her for advice. We have a rapport.

Yet, there's still something holding me back. Sometimes I feel close to both of them, sometimes I don't. My barriers are still up, and funnily enough, even more so with Samantha than with Paula. I think it's because after we'd first met, she started to act in the same way that Karen did. She kept calling me 'my sister' and was phoning me about three times a week. It was all getting a little suffocating and I was worried about the effect it was having on Mum and Dad. If I wasn't in, they'd answer the 'phone and Samantha would start talking to them. I just felt it was unfair on them and I wanted to keep a lid on it, so to speak.

However, I decided to deal with the Samantha situation in the same way I had with Karen – to back away slightly. It has balanced out now and although I feel a little cruel, I have got my own life and I need to consider Mum's and Dad's feelings. Samantha gets annoyed if she feels I'm not contacting her enough and tells me in her letters that she's feeling disappointed and angry. She sometimes threatens to come and visit me and the rest of my family, but I don't want her to: mainly because of the guilt I feel about what I've had compared to her. I also want to keep the two families separate.

Karen now leaves it to me to contact her. She sends me Christmas and birthday cards and seems to accept I have my own life. I had to pull away slowly and perhaps it was slightly unkind, but I think it was better than telling her outright she could never really be my 'mum'. I went to see her and Paul and the others about three months ago. It's more of a friendship than a mother–daughter relationship. She can't have that type of relationship with me and she has accepted that now.

I see the future continuing in the same way, perhaps with me going up to see them all about once a year. I send the children birthday and Christmas cards, but I don't sign them 'Auntie Sue' or anything. My adoptive family come first and always will.

Andrew

I was aware I was adopted at the earliest possible age and that my original name, given at birth, was Mark. My adoptive parents took me under their wing when I was six weeks old and they told me all this. A year and a half afterwards, my parents adopted another boy and he was made clearly aware of his adoption too. My adoptive parents firmly believed that there should be no secrets.

Up until my early teens, the fact that I was adopted didn't really register. I knew I had another mother and father somewhere, but I wasn't really bothered. However, as time went on, it began to play on my mind. There were a few comments from friends and relatives about it all and I remember once that a cousin made a point of asking whether I would like to meet my real parents. I was probably around ten at the time and I recall being a bit cut up by the question, because it made me truly realise for the first time that I wasn't blood-related to my parents.

Shortly after this conversation – maybe when I was eleven or twelve – I made tracks to try and find out something more. I've always had an investigative mind, so I rooted around my parents' belongings and eventually came across a milk token which dated back to the late 1950s. On it was written my real name and surname, as well as my mother's full name and address. Her name was Jean. I removed the token from my parents' stuff and hid it in my room. It went missing a few days later. It was obvious my parents had found it and taken it back.

Unfortunately, I hadn't made a note of my mother's address and I couldn't remember it. So, I made another concerted effort to go through all their paperwork and this time, I found a second item – a coupon book – again with my mother's name and address on it. This time, I hid the book behind a mirror on my bedroom wall, where it proved to be safe. It was good knowing that whenever I needed to, I could contact her, my mother, directly.

My parents never spoke about the milk token or coupon book. I think they must have taken the token back to stop me going to look for my mother. The fact that they never spoke about the incident was indicative of the way I was brought up. It was an extremely strict household and although they were quite open in one sense, their whole ethos was one of 'tough' love. I got hugs only at certain times. This has affected me very strongly and has made me a very cold person.

By the time I was in my early teens, I just wasn't interested in my adoptive family. My 'relatives' – aunties, uncles, cousins – meant nothing to me. As far as I was concerned, they had no connection with me whatsoever. They were nice enough people, but I had no feeling of any link with them. I saw my adoptive brother as a close friend rather than a brother. We were very different: he was extremely good with his hands and was into car mechanics and building things. My forté was totally intellectual.

Anyway, after the milk token business, the question of tracing my parents faded into the background. There the matter rested right the way through until 1985, when I reached twenty-eight. Why I left it that amount of time, I'm not quite sure. But it never really caught my imagination to do anything more up until then. For some reason then, I became sure I wanted to do it. I had established myself as a writer by this stage – my subjects were the occult and landscape mysteries – and I suppose an 'inner quest' of another sort seemed the right thing to do.

I decided, firstly, to find my birth mother. I had no knowledge whatsoever of her predicament when I was born, other than the fact that she had left me in a mother and baby home somewhere near Dunstable in Bedfordshire. I also had her address, of course, which I'd written in my address book, copied from the coupon book I'd stashed away.

I started by working on the premise that my mother was probably young and unmarried when she'd had me. I assumed she was about twenty when I was born. I went to St Catherine's House and found my birth certificate, which gave me details of her parentage and situation when she'd had me. By this time, I was becoming very eager to find out about my ancestral roots – my writing interests were very much based on ancient mysteries and history – and I wanted to know more about my blood lines, so to speak. I then found out that my mother had married a couple of years after I'd been born and that her marital home was also in Bedford, near to the original address I already had. I checked up the local 'phone book and got the 'phone number very easily.

I sat on the information for a couple of days and consulted with some colleagues at the local newspaper where I was working at the time. I asked them what I should do to approach my mother, and, typically of journalists, they suggested a trip to the pub to give me some Dutch courage. So we all traipsed to the pub, downed a few and came back to the office. Then they all stood around while I dialled the number. A young male voice answered the 'phone and said that Jean would be back shortly. I didn't give any details, just my name and surname. I felt safe doing that, because, of course, my name wouldn't mean anything to her. She later told me that she'd known it was me, instantaneously. I suppose you could put some of this down to female intuition, and the fact that she'd known that at some point in her life she'd probably get a call.

I rang back about half an hour later and the same male voice answered. I asked to speak to Jean and suddenly she was there.

'Is that Jean Smith?' I asked.

'Yes.'

'Right, I think you should sit down for this one. My name's Andrew, but you may know me by the name Mark Pirie.' She sounded humoured by what I'd said.

'Well, I could hardly forget you, could I?' her reply came back.

We sat and talked briefly and she sounded very happy. Unfortunately, my manner comes over as quite cold and calculating, so I wasn't showing any emotion. (I was treating it like I'd just discovered the answer to one of the mysteries I write about. The fact that the solution to the mystery was my real mother didn't really make much difference at the time.)

She told me in the course of the conversation that although her husband knew about me, her two sons did not, and that she would have to tread carefully. I didn't really take that in at the time. I was interested in something else.

I said, 'Look, before I put the 'phone down, there is one thing I have to know.' She must have thought I was going to ask about my real father.

'I need to know what time of day I was born,' I continued, 'otherwise I can't get my astrological birth chart done.'

She laughed and told me it was about six or seven o'clock in the morning. Strangely enough, I'd always had a feeling that this was the case: so much so, that I'd previously asked an astrologer to complete my chart on that premise. I was very pleased – my instincts had been right. By the end of the 'phone call, we'd arranged to meet at Jean's sister's home the following week.

Before the meeting, loads of things were going through my mind. What would she look like? What would she be like? What were we going to talk about? Would we get on?

The day came and I drove up to Bedford. I found the house easily and knocked on the door. My aunt and my mother were standing in the hallway. I recognised Jean immediately and went and hugged her. She returned it. That was that. We went into the sitting room and sat down and talked.

What did I feel? The best way I can describe it is that I felt some kind of rapport. There was a definite feeling, some type of connection, but that was as far as it went. It was similar to meeting up with a good friend who you haven't seen for a long time. In other words, you've had connections with them in the past, you've been separated, and those connections, the reasons why you were friends with them in the first place, are still there. I instantly got on with her. Physically, she was much smaller than me, her dark hair was going grey, and there were some similarities, especially when it came to mannerisms. She crossed and uncrossed her legs constantly and had a general, nervous tension about her that I also have.

After the introductions and plentiful cups of tea, we started to talk about what had actually happened. I heard her story, the other side of the coin, for the first time. Obviously, she was prepared for one of my primary questions to be about my father. I wanted to know about him by this stage. (Through my work at the time, I'd come into contact with several psychics, some of whom had told me that I should contact my father as he was unwell.) She broached the subject before I asked and showed me a photo of a six-foot tall, strapping blond young man in US uniform. She told me his name was Theodore, that he had been in the US Air Force and had been stationed in Bedfordshire in the late 1950s. He had been married with children, but had struck up a relationship with her and they had, supposedly, been in love. She'd got pregnant, and hadn't told anyone about it. A few months later, her sister had sussed the situation, confronted her and persuaded her to tell my father. But when Jean tried to contact Theodore, she discovered that he'd been transferred to a 'far-off' place – which turned out later to be the US – and she never heard another word from him. The six-million-dollar question was whether he knew nothing, or had asked for a transfer because he had guessed Jean's situation. She'd never found out.

Once I knew this, we went on to have a really good chat. The conversation was very easy and we talked the whole afternoon. On the way out, we hugged and kissed, and that was it.

A few days later, I telephoned Jean at her home address. Again, she emphasised that her sons did not know anything, so we agreed that we should keep in contact by letter and that I should visit her again soon. Within a month, I was back up there and I met her, interestingly enough, at her mother's – my grandmother's – house, which was the very same address that had been on the milk token so many years before. It was very weird that I should be there, thirty years later. My grandmother turned out to be totally eccentric, and again, there was quite a close connection. As with the first time I met Jean, we got on very well. She and I went out for a drink in a pub and I felt quite close to her. Everything was fine and having spent the whole day there, I returned home. It turned out to be the last time I ever saw her.

During the times when I was meeting Jean, I started to feel guilty about my adoptive parents. I hadn't told them anything, yet I'd also returned back home to live with them for a time. I didn't feel guilty about doing what I was doing, but rather that I had seen my real mother and hadn't told them.

Finding Jean was also having another effect. I was beginning to realise that my adoptive mother was a much stronger and more powerful character than I'd realised before. I was starting to appreciate her more and began to understand what a good woman she was. Her strength and her wisdom were suddenly more apparent. In contrast, Jean seemed scatty, a bit absent-minded even; not in the same strong mould as Mum.

I continued to write to Jean after our second meeting, but the letters from her became less and less frequent. Within six months or a year, they stopped completely. The only contact I had after that was with Gillian, her sister, who kept me in touch with family news. Since then, I've sent Christmas cards every year to Jean, Gillian and my grandmother: simply because I feel I should and to show that I still think about them. It's strange though. For whatever Jean's reasons are for not contacting me, I feel sort of the same – that I don't have any particular need to see her again either. I'd like to have contact by occasional letter, but there seems to be little point in taking things further than that.

I assume that the main reason for her stopping communication was that my re-emergence became a problem. Although she'd told me her husband was happy that she'd found me, I think he had reservations about us communicating intensely. I think both of them wanted to avoid the children finding out. I don't necessarily think this was a good move, but it was and is her decision. However, considering the boys' ages – both were in their early twenties at this stage – I couldn't quite understand why she couldn't put her foot down with them. I did feel slightly resentful about that.

During our first meeting, Jean had asked me to promise that I wouldn't try to contact my father, as he was married and had children. At the time, I had agreed and told her it was no problem. By this time, however, I'd changed my mind. I told myself, 'No, he is my father and I've got to do it.'

I made my first forays by contacting agencies that had links with the US forces and giving them my father's full name, which I had. I also told them that I knew he hailed from somewhere in Michigan. I waited to hear something, but the result was zero. They turned up nothing at all.

I was almost ready to give up and even tried using an Ouija board to locate him. Another psychic told me I should keep trying because Theodore was still unwell. I did for a short while longer, but ultimately, all my efforts failed.

It wasn't until 1995 that, having given up, I made contact with a woman who was using the Internet to find people's birth parents on both sides of the Atlantic. She asked me whether I wanted her to 'put the word out' to her contacts in the States to look for my father. Not holding out too much hope that it would work, I said yes. I didn't think it would get me anywhere.

Within a day of asking me, the woman came back to me and said she'd got someone on the case. Two days later, she came back to me again and said she thought they'd tracked him down. And then, that very same night, she told me that they had found his 'phone number. I was stunned and delighted. It had taken three days.

I plucked up all my courage and went for it later that night. I dialled the number and got a business answerphone, with a female voice on the message. I left my name and number.

I didn't get any response, so I left several more messages over the next couple of days. Still nothing. Things weren't looking good.

Then, a couple of weeks later, and late one night when I was in bed, the 'phone rang. I was still dazed with sleep and an American, drawly voice said, 'Hello, Andrew? This is Todd here.' My brain wasn't prepared, it took me totally by surprise. My first words were, 'Did you know a lady called Jean when you were in England?'

'Yes.'

'And you were quite close to her?'

'Yes,' again.

Then I came out with it. 'Well, I am the product of that relationship. I'm her son.'

He sounded a little hesitant and started asking me questions about when I was born and other details. I can see why he did, because he had no knowledge about me and he could have thought someone was playing a trick.

Eventually, he obviously came to the conclusion that I was genuine. He asked about Jean and I told him I'd been in contact with her. He told me that he had loved her dearly and spoke very highly of her. I was very pleased to hear that. He explained that he had been married when he knew her, but that the marriage had ended some years ago. He also told me that he had a weak heart. The psychics had been right! It was very easy to talk to him and he seemed a good man. I felt I could open up to him. There was a definite bond. It also became clear that he was very interested in staying in contact with me.

A couple of weeks later, I received a parcel from Todd. In it were dozens of photographs of him and his family (I'd found out that I had two half-brothers and one half-sister). He told his children and relatives about me immediately. The most amusing aspect was that once he found out I wrote books, he wanted me to send them over. I did, and everyone seemed to love them.

It's got to the stage now where I speak to him on the 'phone about once every two or three weeks. It's good, because it's obvious that he cares. My brothers and sister call occasionally too – my sister is just four months younger than me, so we feel quite close. They all seem very open about it all and there seems to be no problem. They want me to go out and visit: in fact, my sister says that I should as Todd really isn't in the best of health. I do want to go, but my financial situation precludes it at the moment. When I've got time and money, I will.

It's now been nearly ten years since I met Jean and we still have had no contact. It's possible that my half-brothers, her sons, will find out about me by some means. Sometimes I think that maybe it is in fact best to let sleeping dogs lie. I don't feel an urgent necessity to contact her. I don't think it will necessarily enrich my life. I've concluded that if my brothers don't know about me, then that's that. I've no need to pursue the matter any more. However, I think the non-communication is just the way Jean does things. She shuts things out. But I've got to respect her feelings. However, because I still send Christmas cards, I can't help wondering whether my brothers see them and wonder who 'Andrew' is.

They'll be in their early thirties now and you would have thought that by that age, they would be able to handle it. But maybe it's too late. Perhaps I'll drop a card to Jean at some point saying that I hope she's well and see what she does.

My adoptive mother died six years ago. It's a truism of life that you don't know what you've got until it's gone and I really feel now that she was a wonderful person: a shining light. I think she's moulded my personality a lot. My adoptive father and I now get on well: her death has brought us closer together. He has semi-retired to the south coast, and neither of us have a real urge to meet up any more than occasionally. It's nice to know he's there, but we haven't got a lot in common.

One of the main things that interests me about adoption, however, is how adoptees like me respond to the rest of the world. I have definite behaviour patterns and traits which I put down to being adopted.

For instance, I've always been a very cold character. I recently lived with a girlfriend for five years and she left under a cloud saying I never gave her enough love and that I was unreachable. I believe this coldness comes from the sense of isolation an adopted child feels. I was never really interested in the social world around me and I think it's because I've never really known how to 'bond' with people. I was always aware that my adoptive parents were, ultimately, just two people, two strangers; and all their relatives were the same. Family situations have been meaningless to me. Although my friends have been a kind of substitute for this, they have to be very close friends; and I only have a few of them. I find having a wider circle of 'acquaintances' or casual friends difficult to cope with. I'm just not interested in going around with a group of people.

I also only fall in love with people for about five minutes. After that, I just turn it into a one-to-one friendship or I push them away. Being an author helps me in this isolation. It means I can elevate myself from the normal social round, put up barriers and hide away in my own, safe little world which I've created.

A good example is that, up until the mid-1980s, I would never, ever shake people's hands or hug them unless I really had to. I've never hugged my adoptive brother. And the interesting thing is that he never shakes people's hands, or hugs them, unless he has to. It's the physical contact I have a problem with.

However, since meeting Jean, I've gradually broken this 'armour' down and I'm much better about it now. My live-in girlfriend was also very open and tactile, and that helped me break down the barriers. But my 'coldness' towards the outside world still remains intact. I think it will always be the same. I'm still scared of long-term relationships.

Joy

I feel fine about being adopted. It was the best thing that could have happened to me at the time. When my mother gave me up, it was the mid-1960s and life was difficult, so I was given a good childhood and I've had a very good life.

Mine was a private adoption. I was handed to my adoptive parents, via my biological aunt, in 1965, when I was only a few days old. My adoptive dad was fifty-six at the time, and his age meant that he and Mum couldn't adopt through the National Health Service. My mum was forty and desperate for a child. They had some friends nearby who were distantly related to my birth mother, and the adoption was arranged that way. No money changed hands and it was all done through the courts.

I was told I was adopted at a very young age: I was about three, an age when I suppose I could just about grasp the concept. My parents told me that they didn't actually have me, but that I was 'chosen' and 'special', which meant that I was loved all the more. I was very happy about that and thought how nice it was. So much so, that I used to annoy other children when I met them by saying, 'Hello, my name's Joy and I'm adopted and that means I'm special.' The fact was that I accepted my adoption completely. It made me feel different from other children, but in a nice, rather than a horrible way. I learnt later that it was a proviso of my adoption that my adoptive parents agreed to tell me about my background when I was old enough. It was never to be a big, dark secret.

The one thing I did find difficult was that I was an only child. Although I lived in a lovely house, had wonderful toys, and Mum and Dad gave me lots of attention, I felt very lonely and used to get extremely bored. My poor mum used to have to keep me amused for hours on end: it must have driven her nutty. My best friend, who had three brothers and sisters, lived on the same road, and I adored visiting her because it made me feel part of a large family. We used to pretend we were sisters.

Our house was very quiet. My father was very Victorian because of his age. Although we talked during meals, it was all quite formal. I remember having to listen to the BBC World Service every lunchtime during the holidays. It was a bit desperate for a child aged ten or so. My relationship with Dad was that of a grandfather–granddaughter, although we did love each other deeply.

My mum tried to bridge the generation gap and I was extremely close to her. She was a very lovely lady who gave me everything I could ever have needed in terms of love and attention. She never got angry or raised her voice and was always there for me. However, she was a sensitive person, who although not very physical or tactile, was still very affectionate. To me, she was a saint.

When I was old enough, my parents showed me my adoption certificate which had my adopted name on it. One day, whilst rummaging in our coat cupboard, I found my birth certificate, which gave me my birth mother's name, as I remember, as Eira Elizabeth Fenton-Hughes.

When I was eight, I was sent to boarding school. I didn't want to go, because I was so close to Mum, but I think Dad thought I needed the company. The first few days there were quite exciting, but once the novelty had worn off, I felt utterly miserable. I found the next few years difficult.

I started to think about my birth mother during my teenage years, especially on my birthdays. Dad had told me that she was only eighteen when she'd had me, so I wondered what she was like, how young she was, and how she must have felt about giving me up. I imagined her looking very similar to me: just an older version. I knew that at some stage, she had gone to university, so I assumed she was quite bright, which made me feel quite proud. I didn't think about her that often: I certainly wasn't obsessed. I was busy being a teenager and was on a high and just getting on with things. I didn't really think about my birth father at all. If anything, it was the possibility of having brothers or sisters that occupied my thoughts.

At seventeen, I moved to a boarding school in Scarborough, which I loved. It was a mixed school, in contrast to the previous one. It was during my second year there that my mum died.

I'd gone back to school after the summer holidays and I heard from Dad that Mum had had a breakdown and was in hospital. He asked me to write to her, which I did. I wrote her a long letter all about school and telling her how much I loved her. Soon after, I remember going into the boarding house and the house mistress asking me to go and see her after roll-call. I was taken into her room and the headmaster was there. He sat me down and told me my mother was dead. He didn't tell me how she'd died, just that she had. I later found out that she'd committed suicide in hospital.

Her death was a devastating shock. I grew up overnight. Dad was terribly upset and I went back home to look after him. I suddenly realised that life wasn't just a game and began to look at myself, and my whole life, in more perspective.

I finished school the next year and after a stint at college in Bournemouth, moved to Gloucestershire to be with my father. By this time, he too was very ill. He had leukaemia and knew he was dying.

One day, while we were chatting, he said, 'Joy, I've never really told you this, but I believe that your real mother married your real father – at least, that's what they were planning when we adopted you.' I remember thinking that it was his way of giving me his approval to search for my birth parents.

Shortly afterwards, I married Sean who was an officer in the Army. Soon after I joined him in Munster, Germany, my dad died. I think it was his love for me that kept him going until I was settled. He was a very brave man.

The next few years passed in a complete rush. We were living abroad a lot and there never seemed to be an opportunity to start my search. By 1994, however, we were back in England, and I had had our third daughter, Natasha. As a family, we were more settled and I remember holding Natasha in my arms and wondering how someone could possibly give up their baby. It was also ten years since my mum had died and I felt that enough time had passed for me to begin my tracing. I was very conscious of how my adoptive aunts and uncles would react once they found out I had started to look. By this stage however, I had three children and a good marriage. I felt secure and happy, so I would be able to cope if things didn't go well.

I didn't know how or where to start tracing, so I hired a private detective who said he wouldn't charge me unless he found something out. I gave him my mother's name as Eira Fenton-Hughes and he said he hoped to have something for me within a couple of weeks. Time passed and nothing happened. When I called him, he said he had found absolutely nothing at St Catherine's House and the trail was completely cold. I was very disappointed, but I decided it was perhaps better to leave things for a bit. I told myself that perhaps I was opening up something of a Pandora's box and that it might be better left closed.

In 1995, we moved house again and I made friends with one of my neighbours, Debbie, who was also adopted. She had traced and met her birth mother and father, and told me all about it. She persuaded me to start tracing again and came over the next day with all the names and addresses of the organisations I should contact, including NORCAP (see Appendix).

I rang NORCAP and contacted Wiltshire Social Services. They assigned me a social worker who told me all the risks and possible outcomes. I obtained my original birth certificate and discovered my original name was Helen Joy Minton-Hughes. Minton-Hughes rather than Fenton-Hughes! That's why my detective hadn't found anything! My social worker informed me that my mother had been twenty-one when she'd had me and gave me my father's name. She also said that they hadn't been ready to get married when I was born.

I was very happy, but I did have some doubts. However, I put these aside: I felt it was important from a medical point of view to find out about my background, and I was also very curious. I then got in touch with NORCAP, who helped a lot. I asked one of their researchers for assistance. My husband, Sean, was then posted to Brunei for a few months, and while he was away, my researcher confirmed that my parents had married. I thought 'Wow!' Suddenly I realised that I might have full brothers and sisters, and the thought was hugely exciting. It was the one thing I'd truly longed for. I also thought that if my parents were still married, it would be much easier for them to accept me.

A little later, I learnt that I had two siblings. However, my researcher told me I would have to wait three weeks to confirm whether they were brothers or sisters. I thought, 'Oh hell! I can't wait three weeks!' I was really into it at this stage and everything was going too slow. I was so close to finding out it made the thought of waiting any longer interminable.

I'm very impulsive, so I acted there and then. I found an address on my parents' marriage certificate and discovered there was still someone with my father's surname living there. I rang my counsellor who told me to write to the address. But I couldn't. I had to ring.

I got the number from directory enquiries and dialled it. An elderly lady answered, and I asked where I could get in touch with Richard Eastwood – my father's name. To my amazement, she said she had a step-brother-in-law called Richard who lived in France. She told me he was in his fifties and I knew immediately it was him. I asked whether he was still with Eira. 'Oh no, dear,' she replied, 'They divorced years ago.' I thought, 'Oh no!' I asked her whether they had any children. 'Yes, two.' She then gave me Richard's sister's 'phone number. My aunt! My heart was beating madly.

I rang the number that night and got my cousin. I told her that I was an old friend of Eira and Richard. She told me she'd get back to me. An hour later, the 'phone rang and a man's voice said, 'Hello?' I immediately assumed it was my uncle, my aunt's husband.

'Can I ask why you're trying to contact Eira Eastwood?' he said.

'I'm doing it on behalf of a friend who's trying to find members of her birth family,' I replied. 'She was born in 1965, and I wondered whether you could help.' I don't know how I did it. I deserved an Oscar for my acting.

'Can I ask who you are?' I said.

'I'm Bob Billings,' he replied, 'I'm Eira's second husband.' My heart was in my mouth.

'Can you tell me what date this girl was born?' he asked.

'October 18th,' I replied.

In the background, I heard a Welsh, female voice. 'Did she say the 18th of October?' He said, 'Yes,' and I heard, 'Oh my God!' in the background. I knew it was my mother.

He asked me to tell me more about 'my friend'. I told him and he said that his wife would like to have a word with me. This was it. I knew I was about to speak to my real mother for the first time.

She came on the 'phone and started firing questions at me. I went into auto-pilot: this was my finest acting role ever. I carried on pretending I was the friend, and then asked the question I had to ask.

'Would you be interested in contacting or meeting Joy?' I asked. 'Oh yes', came back the reply. 'It's all I would ever hope for. I'd love to.' I knew I was safe.

'I can't do this anymore,' I blurted.

'Oh, dear, you're not going are you?' Eira said.

'No, I don't mean that,' I said. 'You see, I'm not Joy's friend. I'm Joy.'

Eira just burst into tears and had to give the 'phone back to Bob. I asked them not to be angry with me and explained that I'd pretended so they could back out gracefully if they wanted. Bob said that finding me was something they'd all hoped for.

At this point, I was burning to know about my siblings. Eira came back on the 'phone and told me I had a brother and sister, Nick and Julia. Both had known about my existence for quite some time. I was overwhelmed. I had tears in my eyes and a lump in my throat. Then, amazingly, Julia was thrust on the 'phone. Poor girl! She was only twenty-one. She just said, 'Hello?' in a daze. To break the ice, I asked her how tall she was. 'About five foot four', she replied. 'Oh, well, I must be at the weak end of the gene pool,' I said, 'I'm five foot nothing. And don't tell me, you've got lovely, long, curly hair?' 'Yes,' she said. 'And mine's short and straight,' I replied. And so it went on. We were both laughing.

When I put the 'phone down, I sat on the stairs in disbelief. I couldn't believe I'd spoken to my mother and sister only an hour after making the call to the little old Eastwood lady. I rushed upstairs and tried to explain things to the children. I knew it probably wasn't the best time to tell them, but I had to tell someone. I then made myself a large gin and tonic, downed it one, and sat down in a heap. I rang my in-laws, who were thrilled, but amazed, and then called some of my friends, who were all equally staggered. I was desperate to speak to Sean, but he was in Hong Kong. I managed to get a message to him and he called me back at five o'clock Hong Kong time, ten o'clock English time. 'Hello darling ...' he said and started telling me about his trip. I was so excited, I just said, 'SEAN. JUST SHUT UP AND LISTEN.' I told him everything. He arrived home a few days later very excited for me.

Eira, Bob and I had arranged to meet a couple of weeks later. My immediate reaction was 'Oh no, that's so long away. But I mustn't pressurise them.' However, I woke up the next morning feeling very frustrated. So I sat down immediately and wrote a very chatty, non-pressurising letter, enclosing photos of me, Sean and the kids. I was hoping that once Eira saw the photos, she would want to meet us as soon as possible.

The next day I received a letter from her. It was very long, outlining everything about her life, how thrilled she was I'd got in contact and how she couldn't wait to meet. The next day, I got another letter from her, suggesting she and Bob came up the next weekend and stay in a local hotel, where we could meet. I was over the moon.

The night before, I shut the whole thing out and didn't think about it. But on the morning of our meeting, I was completely a-jitter. The meeting was planned for five that afternoon, so I had the whole day to get through. I was like the proverbial cat on a hot tin roof.

Sean and I drove to the hotel. I was a bundle of nerves and he kept telling me to calm down. The hotel was hosting a wedding reception as we walked in which I thought was very symbolic. I remember looking at the bride with her mother and thinking that could be me and my mother. As we were walking towards Eira's and Bob's room, I kept telling Sean that I wanted to turn round and go. I kept thinking, 'Do I look too fat? Do I look nice?' Eventually, we arrived at the door.

We knocked. Eira answered and gave me a great big hug and started crying. I was too overwhelmed to cry. We walked into the room and Eira hugged Sean. I remember thinking she was never going to put him down. Bob was sitting on the bed and he smiled and put his hand out. We all sat down and made some small talk. After about three minutes, Sean suggested that he and Bob go for a drink in the bar and they left.

Eira and I were alone. I could see some of me in her: the same round face; lovely, friendly eyes; same nose; short in height. I remember being amazed at how well endowed she was, mainly because I'm not! She was also very Welsh. Just like my adoptive mother, who was Scottish, she had a very soft, gentle lilt to her voice.

At first, I felt very odd. Not uncomfortable, just odd, like I was dreaming. 'It's my mum, it's my mum!' I kept saying to myself. She was feeling the same, I know.

To break the ice, I asked her whether she wanted a cup of coffee. We started talking, but it was strange because we were both trying to say things at once. We were both very nervous. Eira then got some photos out which calmed us both down. She showed me pictures of Nick and Julia and my father, Richard. Julia looked just like me but with longer hair. Eira and I talked about the past. She explained how she hadn't wanted to give me away, but circumstances meant she had no choice. Her father had never known she was pregnant and her mother wanted her to finish college. She told me she'd always regretted what she'd done, how hard it had been to do and how she'd thought about me a lot. She'd coped, afterwards, by throwing herself into her studies at university. She and Richard had married two years later and then had Nick and Julia.

After talking about all sorts of things, we joined Sean and Bob for a drink and a meal. Bob had arranged for a bottle of champagne to be at the table which was a lovely touch. I could feel Eira watching me all the way through the meal. I kept snatching glances at her too, but I didn't want to be caught staring at her! Sean kept hugging her and saying to me, 'This is your mum!' We were all laughing and joking, and it was obvious we all had the same sense of humour.

Afterwards, Sean and I drove home. I was exhausted. I hadn't slept properly for a week.

The next day, Eira and Bob came over to our house to meet our three daughters. It was lovely, and the children were very well behaved, for a change! We all went for a pub lunch. Eira loved the children. She'd always wanted grandchildren and Nick later told me how thrilled she was to be a granny. The day went very well.

Eira and Bob had not yet mentioned their visit to me to Nick because they had wanted to meet me first. Once they arrived home though, they rang him immediately. Nick called me that night, saying he had the next day off and would like to come and meet me. He also told me that my father, Richard, was coming to see him and that he could bring him too if that was what I wanted. It was big, second shock for me – I'd thought Richard was in France, where he now lives. I also didn't really know much about him. Eira had been very good in that she had told me very little, saying she wanted me to make up my own mind about him. He'd hurt her very badly, but she didn't want to colour my opinion. I thought that was very noble of her.

Nick was very keen to meet me. He'd actually tried to make contact with me a few years earlier, through my aunt – the one who had looked after me for a few days after I was born – but she'd been sworn to secrecy and had refused to tell him anything. He'd also gone to the hospital where I was born to find out more, but all their records had been destroyed. He told me that all during his childhood, he'd had a feeling that something was missing from the family's life. He had just sensed a missing piece in the jigsaw.

When they arrived, I was very nervous. They came in and just stared at me. They were watching all my mannerisms. I thought my father was eccentric, but in a nice way. He had the same eyes, eyebrows and nose, but what was most similar was his wacky sense of humour. He had longish, wispy, grey hair, like a French artist working in a garret. I remember saying to him, 'You're barking mad.' 'Yes, I am,' he replied. He developed a real affinity with my middle daughter, Emma. She has a funny streak in her, too, and she definitely found a soulmate that day. I really liked Nick. We were both very nervous, but I noticed similar traits. Generally though, the conversation was easy and we all had a nice time.

For the next couple of days, I was a bibbling heap. I couldn't believe what was happening. But I had someone else to meet – my sister Julia. Nick brought her over to meet me. I loved her immediately. I thought she was fabulous. We stood in front of a mirror and smiled, and we looked almost exactly the same. Then, all three of us sat together in the garden, and it was strange, because we all had the same mannerisms and gestures. We then all went shopping. It felt strange being with my brother and sister. It was lovely. There was a real rapport between us.

I'm extremely close to Nick already. He's just as pleased as I am that the 'gap' has been filled. He 'phones me a lot. I feel very close to Julia too, although we don't speak as often, because she seems to be out with her boyfriend a lot! I think Eira's amazed at how well we all get on.

It's all been overwhelming. I've now met my real parents and two full siblings in the space of four weeks. Everyone in my life has been wonderful about the changes. Sean says it's been like being picked up by a tornado. It's affected everyone around me, as if I've thrown a stone into a pond and we all have to deal with the ripples. My in-laws, Sean's parents, for instance, have had to deal with things too. They've been like parents to me over the last few years and up until now, they've been the only grandparents to my children. Now, suddenly, they've had to make way for this new, second set. That must be quite hard for them. But they have been wonderful about

Eira and Richard. They've invited them and us all up to their house in Scarborough for Christmas.

I never really dreamt when I first went into this that I'd be in this situation. Four weeks ago, I merely wanted to get some questions answered and find out what my parents looked like. It's been like winning life's lottery. I think the future looks very exciting and that we're going to go forward from now on. My reasoning is that we've missed thirty years, so let's make up for them and get on with the next thirty. It's a nice feeling. I think it's the best thing I've ever done. I had my doubts, but they're gone now.

My advice to other adoptees is to go ahead, but think seriously about the possible repercussions and consequences. That's important. I was very lucky. I hope everyone else will get as much from their reunions as I have.

Paula

I think I was six weeks old when I was adopted. I was born in Newcastle and my mother, who was nineteen, single, and unable to look after me, kept me for ten days. At that point, I was given to a local couple, who already had two natural children, two girls, who were eight and ten years old. My adoptive mother had suffered a miscarriage with her third child and I think they decided to adopt me as a sort of 'replacement'.

My adoptive mum was forty-three and my dad nearing fifty when they took me on. They lived in quite a pleasant rural area near to Newcastle and were quite comfortably off, although certainly not rich. My father was a postman and my mother a housewife, so they were just an ordinary couple really.

I was around five or six when they told me I was adopted. I remember them saying they had a 'surprise' for me and recall walking up a hill towards home and feeling really excited. I assumed they were going to give me a present, such as sweets or chocolate. They sat me down in the sitting room and explained that my 'real' mother hadn't wanted me and that they'd adopted me as a result. I was also told they had lost a baby and that I was there to help take my adoptive mum's mind off things. Looking back, I think it was a pretty insensitive and negative way to tell me, although I accept it wasn't their fault. They just hadn't known how to handle the situation.

I remember that I didn't really understand what was going on. But I also remember having a strong sense of not 'belonging'. The way they told me has stayed with me, right up until now. If someone tells me they have a 'surprise' for me, it tends to worry and concern me instead of excite me.

As I grew up, my feeling of not belonging remained. I somehow came to believe that being adopted meant paying a price. The price was always feeling the odd one out and being on the outside looking in. I had awful bouts of insecurity, which I kept trying to fight but which wouldn't go away.

To make things worse, my adoptive family weren't loving and open at all, so it was almost like a double rejection. Mum and Dad didn't really express their feelings and were never very affectionate. They never said, 'We love you' or 'We're glad to have you' at any point. Instead, I seemed to be constantly reminded that I wasn't one of them. It became clear that Dad hadn't wanted another child, although he had agreed to my adoption at the time. He could also be quite cruel verbally at times. He once called me a 'bloody Irish creature' (my natural mother came from Northern Ireland), and would often say how he wished they'd never had me.

Initially, my way of coping with all this was to shout back and get upset. I was so frustrated at not having anyone to talk to about it and I felt very unwanted and unloved. Sometimes it all just boiled over. I remember that when we were having arguments, Mum would hide in the garden so she could pretend they weren't happening. This just added to my sense of isolation and loneliness.

As I got older and my awareness of the people around me grew, my feelings of being different became stronger. Other people's families seemed so close and united compared to ours. Mum and Dad seemed so old and never did anything which my friends' families were doing: there were no special days out or holidays. They never seemed to do anything which was family-oriented and, at the time, I connected this to my being adopted. Now I know the two things probably weren't linked. But at the time, I certainly thought I was the cause of this 'inactivity'. It magnified my feelings of being different from my peers.

My two sisters were quite a few years older and were very placid and quiet compared to me. I don't think they really understood me because they didn't know 'who' I was. I sensed that they were always trying to make me more like them, rather than saying 'Hang on, you're different from us and we understand that.' I think they wanted another quiet mouse of a person to mirror them.

I was seventeen when I found a document about my adoption at home. It wasn't a real shock because I knew I was adopted, but it was incredibly strange. It was so weird reading about this baby that was me: it was like reading about a different person. It was marked 'Confidential' and it detailed quite a lot about my birth mother, Kathy: her interests, her parents and the circumstances surrounding my adoption. It also outlined something about my father, who was called Peter, and with whom Kathy had had a short relationship. I kept thinking 'This isn't me,' yet the information about her interests and characteristics was very similar to mine. She liked music, dancing, singing and cooking – all of which I do – and this generated the idea that she was the missing 'jigsaw piece' in my life. She would solve all my problems and complete things. I began to believe that meeting her would make all my hurts better, and that my feelings of being unloved and unwanted would suddenly disappear once she was back in my life. She was my miracle cure.

Light grows dim
Tear-stained, you don't fit in
Feelings blocked from long ago
Hold you back and tell you no
Not good enough
Or so they say
Unwanted, just keep out of the way
That's not how it's meant to be
Open your eyes and you will see.

Follow the truth inside
Know yourself that they lied
Asking who you are
Home is in the heart,
In the heart,
Home is in the heart.

Paula

I'd found the adoption documents when Mum was away, and when she came back, I told her what I'd discovered. She was pretty upset and shocked. I told her that I was going to look for Kathy.

My next move was to contact the Social Services. But after that, for some reason, I decided the time wasn't quite right to go any further. It wasn't the right moment in my life. There were lots of other things happening and I put the idea away for a time.

I left school when I was seventeen, went to college, and then found employment in a series of jobs which I kept for around nine months each time, before moving on. I couldn't really settle into anything, it was as if I was running away from myself. I moved out of home when I was nineteen which was a real relief. Dad had been saying things like, 'Clear off', and 'We don't want you here' for about a year before that. I started a relationship with a guy, Simon, and eventually moved to Darlington to live with him.

On my twenty-third birthday, I had an overwhelming sense that now was the time to find Kathy. At this stage, my relationship with Simon wasn't very fulfilling and I was starting to feel very alone again. I started the search on the actual day of my birthday and telephoned the National Adoption Society there and then. I then contacted NORCAP (see Appendix), who were really helpful, and because I had a lot of information about my natural parents, it was really easy to find Kathy. Ultimately, I contacted the local council, who gave me Kathy's address. My NORCAP counsellor then wrote the famous 'ambiguous' letter to her and I waited to hear back.

I didn't have to wait long. A couple of days later, the counsellor rang me to say Kathy had responded and wanted to meet me. I can't explain how excited I was.

Only a couple of days after that, I was in the sitting room and the telephone rang. I sensed it was Kathy immediately, even though I didn't know NORCAP had given her my 'phone number. Intuition, instinct, whatever it was, I just knew who was going to be on the end of the line.

I picked up the 'phone, she introduced herself, and that was it. We chatted for an hour and a half and I remember a lot of laughter, as if I was talking to an old friend who I hadn't seen for years but still had a strong rapport with. In hindsight, I remember her talking a lot about herself. She explained that she'd loved me so much that she had had to give me up to give me a better chance in life. She also told me that she'd been married twice, but was separated from her second husband and that she was a spiritual preacher, working in spiritualist churches. The whole conversation was strange because it seemed so normal. The other thing that struck me was that she lived only half an hour away from the house where I'd grown up. The realisation that she'd been so near to me hit home. I could have easily passed her in the street, at any time, and not known it. All those years I'd been scanning faces in crowds and one of them could well have been her – my real mother! We got on very well. At the end of the call, we agreed she would send me a photo of herself and that we should meet.

We arranged to meet the next Sunday, and when the day came, her photos hadn't arrived. Simon and I drove to Newcastle and during the journey, my emotions were churning up: I was happy, scared, excited, nervous. I experienced almost every feeling anyone could ever have! I also started to visualise Kathy. Because Simon had convinced me I was overweight, I created this image of her as a hideous-looking, huge woman with a massive, pear-shaped bottom.

When we finally arrived at Newcastle, we stopped to buy Kathy some flowers and the car, without warning, broke down. It just stopped and wouldn't move. I began to panic. Unfortunately, my upset swamped all the other feelings I was having about the reunion, so by the time we arrived at her door, I was in quite a state.

I rang the bell and, within seconds, this tiny woman answered the door. She was small and petite. I was completely taken aback. My immediate thoughts were, 'This can't be my mother, she's too small!' It was like my fantasy had hit reality and I believed the fantasy more than what was staring me in the face. She was about eight stone and wore glasses. Nothing like anything I had imagined. It was only later, when time had passed, that our physical similarities – our eyes are the same – became more apparent. I didn't feel anything in those first moments. She gave me a big hug, but I didn't feel emotional. I didn't cry. I was quite surprised by that.

Simon disappeared to the pub so that Kathy and I could be alone. We went into the sitting room and started chatting. We talked right through the afternoon and evening. It was very strange and wonderful at the same time. We had twenty-three years to catch up on, so it's not surprising we had plenty to say. Yet, we were two people who had never really met before – two strangers. But we had so much in common that we just seemed instinctively to understand each other.

We talked about everything, although again, when I look back now, I can see that it was Kathy who did the vast majority of the talking. She told me about her childhood, how dreadful her life had been, how her parents hadn't been loving (I've since found out from my natural uncle, her brother, that this probably wasn't true). She didn't seem very interested in my side of things, about what I did, or how my family were. She did ask a few questions, however, and I gave her a photo album, which my mum had, very thoughtfully, put together. It was full of snaps of me at different ages. Kathy seemed grateful for that.

The day ended and we said our goodbyes. As Simon drove me back home, I went over and over things in my head. Although Kathy had talked mostly about herself, I felt that, at last I had met someone who was on the same wavelength as me. These feelings were to get even stronger as time went on: I discovered later that Kathy had almost identical tastes and interests. I had always longed to know someone else who understood how I felt, who knew who I was, and who didn't try to make me into a little 'clone' of themselves. Now I had that person: someone with the same beliefs and the same way of thinking.

After our first meeting, we started to write and a couple of weeks later, Kathy came to stay with me and Simon for the weekend. She was good fun: lively, young and modern and she got on very well with our friends. I'd always wanted a young and trendy mum and here she was! However, perhaps there were some signals of future problems, even then. She let me know – either by letter or verbally, I can't remember – that she didn't like Simon. She said she had 'bad' feelings about him. I was, at this time, questioning my relationship with him, but now, in retrospect, I see it as the start of her trying to control my life.

I left Simon a few weeks later and moved nearer to Newcastle to live with one of my adoptive sisters. I got a job in a hotel and began to see Kathy about four times a week. Our relationship became quite intense. We talked about absolutely everything. I was also upset about my split from Simon and was feeling vulnerable and lonely. Kathy seemed to fill the gap. I felt I needed someone to make my decisions for me and she was always there. I was getting dragged into her spiritual beliefs as well. She believed she was clairvoyant and would always give me advice based on what her 'spirit friends' had told her. I guess, because I was insecure at the time, I was attracted to it all. I had also always viewed myself as an intuitive person – I too seemed to pick up 'vibes' from people – so her spiritual beliefs seemed to be yet another connection between us. However, I think now that I was simply overawed by having this new person in my life.

Even so, I remember thinking that Kathy always had something wrong with her. Whenever I visited, she was either ill or depressed or had something to complain about. She seemed totally immersed in herself.

Throughout all this, I was being totally honest with my adoptive family about what was happening. Dad didn't seem to care and didn't really get involved or ask questions at all. I now put this down to the fact that he has a problem with communication: he was interested, but wasn't able to talk about it. Mum was slightly defensive and said things like, 'I suppose you won't want to know us now, because you've got Kathy.' I felt sorry for her, but I felt it was better to be honest rather than go behind their backs.

I'd been seeing Kathy regularly for a few months when things got strained. During one of my visits, she'd told me I had a half-brother, Nicholas, who was a year younger than me and whom she had also given up for adoption. It was a shock, to say the least. Up until then, I'd believed in her reasons for giving me up: that she'd loved me so much she'd wanted to put my interests first. I'd thought, 'Fair enough. People make mistakes and she genuinely thought she was giving me a better life.' Once I knew she'd become pregnant for a second time, just three months after having me, it made everything she'd told me less credible. I believe that if someone really wants a baby that they will do anything to keep it – but Kathy had given up two – however painful it had been. All her stories about loving me and wanting me suddenly seemed hollow.

By early 1993, around six months after our first meeting, I began to feel reluctant about going to see her. I didn't want to hear how ill she felt, what problems she had and what a dreadful state her life was in. I couldn't bear it anymore. It had got too intense and I sensed she was trying to control my life. In hindsight, I wonder now whether she was jealous of me: I was twenty-three, had a good, active life and I'd done lots of different things which perhaps she hadn't had the chance to do.

One of her favourite hobby-horses was telling me that she hadn't had a pleasant childhood and that she, too, had never felt close to her parents, even though she hadn't been adopted. I felt she was trying to trivialise my feelings as a way of resolving her own guilt. She couldn't face up to the problems I had because they pricked her conscience. In fact, whenever I tried to put my own point of view – whether it was about adoption or not – she tended to get upset.

I recall one incident when we were second-hand shopping in Newcastle. Kathy started to criticise her sister – my real aunt, whom I had recently met – suggesting that she was an alcoholic. She started to go over the top and I thought, 'Hang on, if she truly was an alcoholic, you wouldn't be talking so loudly or so horribly about her. You'd be concerned.' I asked her to stop and questioned why she was talking about her sister in that way. Her reaction was melodramatic. She flew into a tantrum and stormed off down the road. It was the first time that I stood back from the situation and thought, 'Wait a minute, this isn't right.'

It was at this point that I decided that I wanted to change my life. I was offered the chance to go to the USA for a year, as a nanny. The part of me that always wanted to move on and leave the past behind was resurfacing. The whole process of applying for the job, getting it, and flying out was extremely quick: two months later, I was on my way. I told Kathy about my plans, but she seemed to play down the importance of it. I was so excited, and I wanted her to be as excited as I was. But she wasn't.

My first job in the States didn't work out. The family was very negative, so I was unhappy from early on. I turned to

Kathy when I was miserable and called her several times when I was feeling low. We wrote to each other regularly. She was very supportive, telling me all her psychic feelings about the situation I was in. I think she was enjoying the drama of it all. Finally, after about two months, the family agreed that things weren't working out, and I moved to a second family.

This time, things were much better. As time passed and I grew happier and made new friends, my letters and contact with Kathy slowed down. I'd had a $220 'phone bill with my first family because of all my calls to England, so I knew I had to limit my spending. But Kathy started to get upset. She began writing letters asking why I wasn't 'phoning her and suggesting it was simply because I was happier and therefore didn't need her as much.

By this stage, I was beginning to question my whole life. I'd been on a roller coaster of emotions and events, I was facing up to the fact that I was blocking out all my problems rather than dealing with them. Maybe it was my being in the States, where people are much more open about their feelings.

The next letter I received from Kathy started things off. In it, she said she hoped that she hadn't blighted my life by giving me up. I decided that this time around, I was going to be totally honest with her. I wrote back and explained that when I'd first met her, I hadn't felt resentful. But I also questioned whether she had 'really wanted' me. I suggested she was trying to absolve herself of her guilt by convincing herself that she had loved me and wanted me, when in fact, she hadn't. I guess I was on a 'honesty kick'. It was an almost uncontrollable need to get everything off my chest.

I should have seen it coming, but I got the most horrible letter back. She called me selfish and critical and claimed I couldn't possibly understand what she'd gone through. She also said that I'd tried to control her when we'd first met. I was very hurt. She continued to write letters in the same vein and I decided to stop writing back. I don't know whether that was right or wrong; I just thought it best to be silent. I didn't want to write anything hateful or abusive back.

I came back to England a year later. I telephoned Kathy to say 'Hello', but decided that I would keep my distance initially. Her birthday was two weeks later, and I went out and bought her a card and present. Unfortunately, I forgot to post them on time and she called me on the day to ask where they were. I told her that I'd forgotten to post them and apologised. She then got abusive, calling me thoughtless and selfish, and slammed the 'phone down. I called her back and told her never to speak to me like that again. I hate getting into conflicts with people, because I'm so scared of rejection. Instead, she shouted at me again. After that, we didn't speak for a week. By this time, though, I started to feel guilty, so I called her back to apologise for making her feel bad.

We didn't contact each other for eighteen months after that call. However, I stayed in contact with Tony, Kathy's brother, whom I had met and become friendly with in the first few months after our reunion. I saw him and his wife regularly, and one day, he told me I should think about making friends with Kathy again. I started to think he was right, so I called her the next day. She was really excited and we arranged to meet up with Tony for a meal the next evening. Everything went smoothly and Kathy and I met a couple more times and got on very well. We chatted a lot and I began to feel we could pick up from where we'd left off.

The last time we saw each other was when she invited me to dinner at her home. Everything was going well until she started talking about a birth mothers' group she'd joined. She recounted to me how, during a group meeting, she'd stood up and told everyone how dreadful it had been to give me up and how many sacrifices she'd made. Apparently, she'd also equated giving up a child for adoption with losing a child through death – on a par with bereavement. She also told me she wanted to trace my half-brother Nicholas.

All my feelings of resentment suddenly came flooding back. I was very angry about her wanting to contact Nicholas, as I thought that she didn't have the right to just walk back into his life. However, I stopped myself from saying anything. I wanted to keep a lid on things. I simply left.

I was due to meet her the next weekend, but couldn't face it. I called her and told her a little white lie, but she obviously didn't believe me. Over the next few days, she called me several times, but I didn't respond.

A few days later, I received a Recorded Delivery letter from her. In it, she said she felt that it wasn't right for me to ignore her. She also wrote that if I didn't want to see her, I should tell her and that she would 'let me go' and would understand. I decided not to respond as I thought it was a bit strange. Again, I just wanted things to cool down.

When I didn't respond, Kathy started to call me again. I was out a lot at this stage, and kept missing her. She left a message on the answerphone telling me the situation was ridiculous and demanding that I call her. I decided that I didn't want to communicate with her: I didn't want to deal with it all.

Two days after that, I received a letter from her solicitor. I was amazed and horrified. In short, it accused me of being abusive to her and of being abusive about her to third parties, meaning Tony. It then warned me not to contact her in any way, for any reason, as it caused her distress; and also warned me to refrain from making contact with my grandparents, Kathy's mother and father, whom I had got to know on the 'phone. The letter was extremely hurtful and I felt incredibly churned up. I felt that it was she who had abused me, and I was extremely angry about being disallowed from contacting my grandparents.

After I'd calmed down a little, I began to realise that the letter was Kathy's way of having the 'last word'. She was terribly hurt that I hadn't responded to her calls, and had effectively turned the situation around to make me look as if I was the one at fault.

The letter arrived in March 1996 and since then I've had no contact with her. I don't know what will happen in the immediate future, but because I now work in Newcastle, I could bump into her in town at any time. I've driven past her house a couple of times, just out of curiosity, but I've never yet been overcome by the urge to contact her again. I don't want her to control my life again. Maybe, however, if she had a change of heart and came to me and said, 'Look, I'm sorry that I gave you up for adoption, I'm sorry that I didn't understand and I'm sorry that I didn't listen to you,' then we could get things sorted out. I suppose there was just never any real acknowledgement from her of what I'd been through.

I don't regret searching for or finding her, however. I had to find her, because I didn't who I was. I was a person that seemed to have come from nowhere. I had no links with the past.

Although part of me now wants to trace my father, I don't feel that I will. For one thing, Kathy didn't ever really talk about him much, so I don't have much information about him to start a search. But I'm scared that if I did find him, it could make matters worse. I can't face a double rejection.

The person that I would like to contact now is my half-brother, Nicholas, who will be twenty-six by now. He's probably in the same area, but his name will have been changed and under current laws, I cannot trace him. All I know is his date of birth.

I don't miss Kathy. But I do feel that finding the missing part of my life I so desperately wanted to know about didn't solve anything. It's like a crystal with a chip in it. The glass is cracked and I used to feel the missing 'chip' would make everything perfect again. I found the chip, but it didn't fit.

However, I've now come to realise that your 'family' aren't necessarily those people who you are related to by blood. I see my 'family' as the people who accept and love me for who I am.

Michael

The hard truth that adoptees face is that searching and finding your parents can, potentially, lead to a lot of heartache. Luckily, I've weathered the storm, but that doesn't mean to say that my reunion experience might not have been very damaging for all the parties involved. My advice to adoptees is to seek professional help and guidance before they start to trace. And even if they don't want to do that, to make sure that they have at least one close friend who can help work through all the issues with them and provide support. It's important, as you never know quite what is going to happen.

My story is quite painful. I was adopted when I was about a year old by a childless couple. He was a police officer and she was Polish, a very domineering woman. From an early age, I can remember that she resented my presence, especially when, later on, she went on to have two natural children.

I suppose life was OK as I grew up. I always knew I was adopted. If my parents hadn't told me, I would have found out for myself anyway, because I had a habit of sneaking around and looking in drawers where I wasn't supposed to look.

When I was about eight or nine, I came across my adoption documents, which listed my birth mother's name – Josephine O'Geary – and mine, Michael O'Geary. Pure Irish. Finding all this information out didn't upset me. In fact, I felt rather special and grand about it all.

As I got older, although I had security, I had no love or affection whatsoever from my adoptive mother. To this day, I don't recall ever being held, kissed or cuddled by her – ever – and in fact, I've never known what it is like to be held by a woman. When my younger sister arrived, all my mother's affections – what little there were – were transferred from me to Geraldine, the baby. And when my younger brother, Neil, arrived (I was ten years old at the time), I remember feeling particularly bereft and alone.

My mother was always very cold and distant towards me, although she was much more giving and tactile towards my brother and sister. She could also be very cruel. I remember that once she told me, 'You have no more right to be here than the cat.' She would slap and kick me every day. On a couple of occasions, I can remember nearly turning on her. Yet, there was a saving grace for me, in that I'd always had this rather haughty attitude about myself, even as a child. The bottom line for me was, 'Actually, you can't touch me.' My mother knew it and I think that made her resent me more.

I still harbour some angry feelings about her treatment of me, but I've just had to come to terms with them over the years. I am gay, but I don't put it down to the lack of maternal love. I see it as something quite separate, despite what certain schools of thought believe. I know my sexuality has always been within me, not grafted on from the outside.

In contrast to my mother, my adoptive father was very much more caring and tactile. He was, quite simply, the best dad anyone could ever ask for. Although he had to discipline us when we misbehaved, he was always very affectionate. I felt a lot for him.

In fact, I remember one day, while he was at work, I went into the front garden and hugged the tree that was there, clasping it with both arms, thinking it was him. I used to wait for him to come back home after work. When he did, I'd make a beeline for him and, more often than not, burst into tears. This would usually spark off a row between him and my mother, as he would ask why I was crying and what she had done to me during the day.

Being adopted meant I could fantasise about the mother I didn't know. I imagined my natural mother as a huge-hipped, rosy-cheeked woman running around making cakes all the time: very homely, very loving and very motherly. The exact opposite of my adoptive mother in fact. My fantasy was that my real mother was a wonderful person, and that once I'd found her, everything would be hunky dory. I had these fantasies right through my teens, but although I thought about finding her, I never did anything about it.

It wasn't until my adoptive father died, in my mid-twenties, that I first started seriously to consider searching. It was then that I knew I had to trace my real mother, find out who I was, where I came from. By this time, I was working as a psychiatric nurse and I applied to Somerset House for my birth certificate. I was put on to a Social Services counsellor, who filtered through more details to me.

However, at this point, things were happening in my life and I stopped. Another ten years or so passed before I took up the search again. I had settled in Brighton and I felt the time was right. I spoke to a NORCAP counsellor (see Appendix) who urged me to arrange counselling during my tracing.

I had the basic details about my mother, and even more usefully, I had an old tea-towel which listed all the clans in Ireland and where they hailed from. I found that the O'Gearys had been rich landowners in Donegal, so I went to the public library and looked up the name in the Donegal telephone directory. I then simply picked numbers from the list I had made and started ringing them direct.

I think I made about ten calls before I struck gold. The man who answered turned out to have been at school with my mother. He told me he knew her and her sister, and that the family had emigrated to New York. He also told me that one of my mother's brothers, Charlie, ran one of the biggest Irish pubs in the city. He asked me to call him the next day, and when I did, he enquired why I wanted to know more about the family. I was very cautious about answering, but he'd already put two and two together. 'Are you her son?' he asked. He then asked me whether there was any money in it for him!

I went back to the library and looked up all the microfiche telephone directories for New York, searching for Irish pubs. I found one and 'phoned the number. 'I'm trying to trace Josephine O'Geary,' I said. 'That's my sister,' came the reply. It was my Uncle Charlie and you could hear his brain working overtime.

Eventually, I said, 'I'm awfully sorry about this, but this will probably come as a complete shock to you and I apologise for any disruption or embarrassment it may cause. I have reason to suspect that Josephine is my mother.' Uncle Charlie garbled something about how he needed another drink. He hadn't known anything about me.

He gave me her 'phone number immediately. I felt terribly tingly and excited, but also very cautious as I didn't know anything about her situation. I waited twenty-four hours to collect my thoughts.

I made the call the next afternoon. 'Is that Josephine O'Geary?'

'Who wants to know?' came the reply. I realised Uncle Charlie hadn't told her.

'Well, my name's Michael,' I said. She started hyper-ventilating. She knew. 'I'm very sorry to say this in this way, I wish it could be easier, but I believe I'm your son,' I gulped. I felt so sorry for her at that moment, poor woman. She was incredibly shocked.

'Look, I just want to tell you that I'm alive, well and happy and that it's a great pity that circumstances have prevented us from being together,' I explained. I then gave her the option of stopping the rollercoaster right there and then: if she wanted, I could put the 'phone down and she would never hear from me again. She replied that she did want contact and asked me to send a photograph.

'This is very embarrassing,' she explained. 'I'm married, I have six children – three of them married and a fourth getting married next year – and nobody knows about you.' None of her family knew anything. She had been totally alone when she had given birth to me.

It was a quick call. I felt exhilarated, yet frightened for her. It was clear from our conversation that she'd never expected me to get in touch. I think she thought she was untraceable.

I sent her my photo, along with a letter, care of Uncle Charlie at the bar. It wasn't long before I got a letter back. It was wonderful receiving it. In it, Josephine 'introduced' herself and told me she was expecting me to give her piece of my mind for abandoning me. Her guilt shone through her words. To reassure her, I wrote back saying there was no way I would do anything like that. I'd never felt any resentment towards her, after all. If anything, I'd felt the opposite: I'd always felt incredibly sorry for her.

We exchanged more letters and she told me that she'd informed her husband, my stepfather, who hadn't known a thing about my existence. He had been completely accepting and had 'phoned up all their children one by one and said, 'You've got a new brother.' All of them had been equally receptive and very excited that they had this half-sibling in England whom they knew nothing about. My brother-in-law later told me that, at the time, I was the talk of the town.

The next Christmas Day I spoke to every single one of the family, including my sisters and brothers, on the 'phone. They're all younger than me: Michael, Bernadette, Margaret, Gary, Paul and John. I remember it as a wonderful time. I was incredibly happy. Josephine said it was the best Christmas she'd ever had. My siblings started writing to me and all said they'd never seen her so happy.

My one problem at this stage was whether to tell the family I was gay. They were all Catholics, of course, which made things worse. But Josephine had already spotted something. In one of her letters, she referred to the fact that I'd never mentioned a woman or girlfriend in my life. I simply ignored this approach and didn't say anything. A good friend of mine at the time told me that I was storing up trouble by not telling her.

Not long after, I received another letter saying that as she'd never been able to do anything for me before, she would now like to pay my fare to New York so I could visit. I was out there by April the same year. When I got off the plane, Michael recognised me straight away, and I thought I saw Josephine in the distance. I went up and hugged her, but cautiously. She was quite cautious back. Although I'd seen photos of her, it was amazing to see her in the flesh. She looked very much like me: the hair, eyes and nose were all the same. It was an incredible feeling, knowing someone looked like me. I don't think anyone else but adoptees can understand it.

We went to Josephine's house where the whole family was waiting for me with open arms. I was absolutely shattered from the flight and so overawed by everything that I don't remember much about what was said or how I felt. The evening just passed by in a whirl.

I ended up staying two weeks. The whole visit was incredible. Everyone was very open and welcoming and curious about me. I think they must have noticed I was effeminate, although nobody ever said anything. I decided not to bring up the subject of my homosexuality at all. Throughout my life, I'd never felt the need to make a statement about it, so I reckoned it was up to them to ask. If they had done, I would, of course, have said yes. Besides the issue of my sexuality though, everything was wonderful. I regarded them all as my family and I got the same vibes back.

Once I got back to England, we all continued to write to each other regularly. Then, a few months later, I started to get rather peculiar – in fact, horrible – letters from Josephine. The first asked me whether my relationship with my friend – the man I was living with at the time – was gay. She went on to say that all the family 'hated' gays and that she believed in Adam and Eve, not Adam and Steve.

I was devastated. It was a huge letdown. I thought that I'd had a rapport with her and now it seemed that maybe I hadn't after all.

I was completely open and honest in my letter back. I said that yes, I was gay, but that my relationship with my partner was loving, caring and monogamous. Her reply was softer. She said she was disappointed, but that she wished me all the best in the world, as she always had. But her letters continued to focus on the subject and there was a lot of to-ing and fro-ing about it all. Eventually, I decided to put my foot down. I wrote saying I was sick and tired of all her letters being full of anger and resentment towards me. I said I had no time for it all and wanted to concentrate on the positive things between us. If she didn't want to do that, then we might as well stop contacting each other.

Her letters stopped, although I did receive a couple of Christmas cards from her over the next two years. As far as I was concerned, this behaviour was below the belt. So the next time I received a letter, I didn't respond. More letters arrived, but I still didn't put pen to paper.

At this stage, I was still writing to Anna, my aunt, and Fran, my sister-in-law. They were breaking their hearts over the split between me and Josephine, and had both told me to hang on in there and not give up. They saw it for it what it was: Josephine was simply in denial.

About a year later, I got a scholarship to spend two weeks at a medical college in Georgia in the US. Fran and Anna were delighted and after my two weeks of study finished, I travelled to New York. I stayed with Fran and didn't let Josephine know I was there. A few days later, there was a family birthday party and I went, knowing Josephine was still in the dark. My approach was that either she accepted the agenda on my terms, or she didn't. She arrived and immediately told Michael that I should pack my bags, move out of Fran's and go and stay with her. In my eyes, she had accepted me. I moved to her place.

However, it became clear that she still had a major problem with my sexuality. I still felt undercurrents. The excitement and the fantasies of our first meeting had worn off to a large degree, and here we were having to face up to the stark reality. Her own flesh and blood was gay and she was struggling to come to terms with it.

During my time there, we didn't talk about the subject at all. She simply wasn't open to suggestion. If she had given me pointers to discuss my lifestyle, we could have sat down and had an interesting dialogue and cleared the air, without getting angry or personal. But it just didn't happen. She couldn't raise the subject, so I felt I couldn't either. She's a very powerful personality and I think she liked to see herself as the mother figure of all the family. My being gay was a shaming thing, a huge disappointment.

After my return home and over the next four years, things between us were reasonable. At the beginning, she didn't really write much, but we maintained an irregular correspondence. However, her whole behaviour towards me was something of a thorn in my side.

It got to a point last year when I decided to do something. My live-in relationship had finished and I felt that I needed a break. I flew to New York for a week and again stayed with Fran who always made me feel very welcome. Josephine didn't know I was going until a couple of days before. A few days after arriving, I met her in Fran's house and she was very congenial.

The breakthrough came when, at one of the family get-togethers, Josephine asked me how my partner was. I was taken aback and told her that we'd split up. Her jaw dropped and her eyes lit up. 'Yes,' I said, 'We finished quite some time ago.' Her face was an absolute picture. She was pleased, surprised, flabbergasted and delighted all at the same time. I thought it was terribly funny and that she was terribly silly for wasting all that time. If I'd been upset about the break-up, I suppose I would have felt differently.

Since I've returned home, everything has been very good. We speak on the 'phone about once or twice or month. Our relationship has been transformed. In fact, she came over to England last summer and stayed with me of her own volition. She asked me when I was 'coming home' – in other words, New York.

I hope we can continue in the same vein in the future. A very wise old lady said to me a few years ago that when children reappear after a very long time, things can never be quite the same, and that parents have to accept that their children have changed and have become individuals. I think that sums up my story.

I'm very pleased that I stayed the course with Josephine. I don't regret it and I'm sure she doesn't either. I think every adoptee has that urge and that right: to find out your background, and who made you. But it sometimes needs to be worked on. The need to know your roots is very powerful.

Katie

I was born in Costa Rica and adopted when I was nearly three by an English couple who brought me back to the UK. I was their only child.

They told me I was adopted even before I really understood English. Obviously, I didn't grasp the meaning of it, but I remember my adoptive mum had a book on adoption which she read to me quite a few times as I got older.

The fact that my parents weren't my biological parents only started to sink in during my school years. I realised I was different from everybody else, not only because I was adopted but because my skin was a different colour. There were a few other children in my year at school who were adopted, so that helped.

I was in my teens when I first began to understand fully. I would sometimes resent the fact that I was adopted and would wonder why I hadn't been able to stay in Costa Rica. If I got cross or had an argument with my parents, I'd ask them why they had bothered to adopt me, or why they hadn't adopted another child as well as me so I could have a brother or sister. I didn't like being an only child and was envious of my friends who had siblings. I've always wanted a younger sister or brother.

My adoptive parents, especially my dad, were also quite a bit older than my friends' parents. I found that quite hard. My friends' mums and dads seemed to do much more with them, like having family days out, while my father couldn't join in things as much, although we did have a number of enjoyable family holidays together. Generally, I got on with my parents well, although I was much closer to my mother than my father.

In my teens, I began to think much more about my birth mother. I didn't know at first whether she was alive or dead and I wondered where she was, what she was doing, and whether she'd had any more children after me. The idea of having a family of my own was also very powerful: I really wanted a child of my own – perhaps more so than usual – because of my background. I wanted something that was mine.

My parents often explained my Costa Rican connection and frequently showed me where it was on the map. I didn't have any memories of my time there or the country itself. All I knew was that it was too far away for my liking.

I was always very open with Mum and Dad about the possibility of finding my mother. I think they expected me to want to find her and seemed happy about it, so I never felt guilty. By the time I reached sixteen, I was ready to find her. I knew there was something missing in my life: it felt like a jigsaw that hadn't been completed. I didn't really consider the idea of building a relationship with her at that point, I just wanted the questions I had in my mind answered; to know she was alive and well, and what she was doing in her life. I didn't know much about her at all. We had some idea of her name, that my father hadn't been around when I'd been put into the children's home, and that I had two sisters, one of whom had also been adopted. We didn't know anything about the whereabouts of the other. I was also aware that my mother had not given me up by choice, but that her financial situation and difficult relationship with our father had meant that she had been unable to care for us.

My mum was very supportive and was there for me throughout the search, right from the start. It was all very daunting at the beginning. We didn't really know what to do. The first thing we did was to write to 'Surprise, Surprise', the ITV programme with Cilla Black. But we didn't have enough information for them to trace her, so it got nowhere. Our next step was to write direct to the home in Costa Rica from where I'd been adopted: the Patronato Nacional De La Infancia, in San José, the capital. We wrote several letters over a matter of months, but got no reply at first. When they eventually did respond, they weren't very keen about giving out any information and were generally unco-operative. Eventually though, they wrote back and asked me to send a notarised letter from my solicitor. That didn't work either.

We then asked the International Social Services. in London for help. They wrote to the Patronato on our behalf and we struck lucky. A letter from the home gave us more information about my family – my mother's full name, and the fact that, rather than two sisters, I had two older brothers. I was very surprised, naturally – but to be honest, it didn't really make much difference to my feelings about them. I learnt that one brother had been adopted by a family in the US and that the other, the elder, called William, had stayed in Costa Rica.

Some time later, we received an address for William. He had also been given our address and he wrote to me via the International Social Services, who translated his letter from Spanish into English. Before that, the Social Services sent me photos of him and informed me he was disabled and in a wheelchair. This worried me greatly. I was concerned about whether he was OK, and what was wrong with him. When I received the photos, I saw vague similarities between us –

although my friends and family all said he looked like me. I started up a correspondence with him, getting my letters translated into Spanish as he spoke no English. We wrote a lot, telling each other about our lives. He sent me personal items of his, including a medal he'd won in the Paralympics.

He also sent me a photograph of our mother. It was not all that flattering; she looked a lot older than I'd expected, but I put that down to the fact that she'd had a hard life. William didn't say a lot about her: just that he saw her sometimes but couldn't get to see her more as she worked so hard. I couldn't write directly to her as she couldn't afford a post office box address, so I sent her messages via William. I received messages back from her saying she was very grateful to the Lord that he had brought us back together again and so glad I was alive and well. There was no mention of my father at all and I felt very awkward about asking either her or William about him.

From quite early on in our letters, William and I talked about how we wanted to see each other and that I should go to Costa Rica. I really wanted to, but wanted to take my adoptive mum, who had been a huge support to me. So we had to save up for two air fares, which took us over a year.

I was twenty-two by the time we could afford the trip. The main reason for the visit was to meet William, but I hoped very much I would meet my mother too. However, there was no absolute certainty that this was going to be possible.

We went ahead and booked the flight. I was full of mixed feelings: elation, nerves, apprehension. The flight had a stop-over in Amsterdam, and when we got there, the airline informed us the plane to San José had been over-booked, so we would have to wait another day for the next flight. I panicked and got very upset. I was terrified we would never get there and couldn't stop crying. Eventually though, we got on the right flight.

We arrived late in the evening. It hadn't been possible for William to meet us as he lived some miles from the airport, so we took a cab to our hotel. I felt very strange about the country. Even though I'd spent my earliest years here, I didn't feel at home. Costa Rica just seemed like any other foreign country.

The next day, a lady from the Social Services drove us to meet William. He lived in a church-run sheltered accommodation complex for disabled people. When we arrived, someone said, 'That's your brother over there.' He was wheeling his wheelchair along a path outside his room. I ran over to him and gave him a hug. He looked very delicate, so I was nervous about hugging him too hard. I used the few words of Spanish I knew to say hello and ask how he was. That's all I could say.

I couldn't believe that after more than twenty years apart, we were actually together and that he was sitting in front of me. He was very happy and kept thanking God for bringing me to him. One of the first things I did was to take his hand and check his fingers. I've got double-jointed fingers you see, and I had always wanted to know whether it ran in the family. His fingers weren't like mine – they weren't double-jointed.

William didn't speak any English, so communication was slow. We talked through the interpreter which made things hard as we couldn't express ourselves spontaneously. But I knew that I loved him, perhaps because we had got to know each other through our letters. Over the next few hours, we pored over lots of photographs of when he was younger and some of our mother. I also found out why he was disabled. Apparently, it was a form of non-malignant cancer that can affect people in different ways. His had affected his spine which made walking impossible. I later found out that this was a genetic problem that ran in our family.

We arranged to go back to see William a couple of days later with the plan that my natural mother would be there too. Before the meeting, I can remember being very churned up: exhilarated, but nervous as I didn't know how she'd react. I couldn't wait to see what she looked like in the flesh and all the questions I wanted to ask her raced through my mind.

The day came. One of William's friends had agreed to act as an interpreter. I remember that my mother was late in arriving and I was terribly worried she wouldn't come. We all waited outside, at the end of a long gravel path that led from the complex to the main road. After a few minutes, a tiny figure, hand in hand with a small child, appeared on the horizon. 'That's our mother coming now,' William said. I watched her as she walked towards us. The tension was almost unbearable. She came over and hugged me straight away. She held me so tight I could hardly breathe; she almost squeezed the life out of me. She cried and cried. I returned the hug, but didn't cry. It was weird: she seemed so much more of a stranger than William had. She praised the Lord and then hugged my adoptive mother, saying how grateful she was I had been looked after so well. I was surprised at how they reacted to each other and how well they got on.

Looking at my birth mother, my first feeling was astonishment that she was so tiny. She was minute, perhaps only about four feet ten in height. I scanned her face trying to identify similarities, but she simply didn't look like me. I was a little disappointed.

We all went and sat in William's room and swapped photos again. Again, conversation was difficult because of the language barriers. I was also quite stuck for words. We started with basic conversation and I found out she was employed in a canning factory and worked very long hours. The little boy who was with her was her foster-child. He had been left on her doorstep as a baby and she'd decided to 'adopt' him. I asked her questions about our family: whether she had other relatives, or any other children. She replied that her mother was still alive – my grandmother – and that she also wanted to meet me. I didn't in the end, as the arrangements were so complicated. But it was nice to know I had a grandmother.

I decided not to ask my mother about why she'd given me up. I knew she had had no choice and I didn't want to upset her by bringing it all back again. However, I did tentatively ask her and William about my father. I got the impression it was a sore subject and they glossed over it. They told me he was no longer alive. I still wanted to know more, but felt frightened about asking any more questions. I discovered later that he'd come in and out of my mother's life and had ended up an alcoholic. Apparently though, he had always been very loving and good to me, his only daughter. I was sad that he'd died as I would have liked to have met him.

I saw my mother a few times more after that. William, Mum and I paid her a surprise visit one afternoon. We waited outside her house when she was due back from work. She was delighted to see us, gave me another big hug and took me up and down the road introducing me to her neighbours. She was so proud of me and looked incredibly happy. People started to pop round to her house to take a look at me.

She asked Mum and me round for lunch the next day. The visit was quite difficult for all three of us, because this time round we didn't have an interpreter and had to rely on sign language to communicate. She had obviously gone to some trouble to prepare lunch, which consisted of a meat course, followed by rice pudding (which I hate!). She showed us around her house, which was very small and basic, but extremely clean and tidy. She was obviously very houseproud. There was basically just a sitting-dining area and a bedroom. The bathroom was outside. She mothered me a lot while we were there. I had long hair at the time and she picked up a hairbrush and started brushing it. She also put make-up on my face. I felt a little uncomfortable about it all, but I let her continue because I knew she'd missed out on all that and it was very important to her. She also gave me a present – a big fluffy white teddy bear.

We stayed in Costa Rica for four weeks and I saw her four times in all. By the end of my stay, I still hadn't noticed any real similarities, but I felt quite close to her. I'd also developed a great respect for her. During one of our last meetings, she asked me whether I would stay and live in the country to be near her. I had to say no, which was very hard for me. I don't remember how I actually said it, but I felt very bad about upsetting her. The truth was, however, that Costa Rica still felt very strange to me and there was no way I wanted to leave Mum.

Even so, when it came to the time for us to leave, I didn't want to go. I was desperate to stay longer. At first, we arranged for my mother and William to come to the airport with us, but I decided I couldn't cope with that. They came to San José instead and we all had tea at our hotel. The goodbye was awful. I hugged William and my mother with more feeling than I had ever had before. My emotions hit me very hard. I was in floods of tears. It was very sad for all of us, as we didn't know when we would see each other again. We could write, but it would never be the same. One of the last things they asked me to do was to find Cory, our middle brother, the one who went to live in the US. It was easier for me to do it than for them.

When I got home to England, I was depressed for around two months. Since then – three years ago – I haven't been back to Costa Rica. I want to go, particularly as I now have a son of my own, Samuel. I still write to William and he passes on messages to my mother. She's very excited about being a grandmother. Both her and William are very proud about Samuel, and very keen to meet him.

I have met my brother Cory. When I got back to England, I contacted the International Social Services and with their help, I managed to get Cory's name and his adoptive family's name and address in the US. We approached him via his parents, who told him about my search. Cory then gave the International Social Services his telephone number, which I received several months later. I was very excited, not only for me, but for my mother and William. We'd done it! I let them know immediately and they were over the moon.

I had to wait to make the 'phone call because of the time difference. When I picked up the 'phone, I was practically shaking with nerves. Someone answered the 'phone and I said, 'Is Cory there please?' 'Yes, speaking,' came the reply. 'Cory, it's your sister Katie in England.'

He was amazed and couldn't believe what was happening. I don't think he knew what to say at first. I was surprised by his American accent. I couldn't believe it was really him. He was going out that evening, so our initial call was short. He called me back later and we spoke for about two hours. It was wonderful for me: he was the first blood relative I had met who spoke the same language! I didn't feel close to him straight away though. We talked about when he could come over to England and see me. After the call, we started to write and 'phone each other quite often, which was nice. I gave him William's address and vice versa, and they started to contact each other.

Cory came over to England in 1994 and stayed for four weeks. I went to the airport to meet him by myself. Even though I had seen photos of him, I was worried we wouldn't recognise each other when he came through from customs. I got to the airport very early and had to fill in a lot of time. Again, I was incredibly nervous. He came through, recognised me instantly, and we hugged over the barriers. I was deliriously happy to see him and it was a fantastic feeling being able to talk to him in the same language, one to one. It made such a difference.

I was very proud of him during his stay and we had a lovely time. We got on well and talked until the early hours practically every night. He told me much more about Costa Rica and our early years there, as he hadn't been adopted until much later than me.

A few months later, I visited him in the US. It was then that things started to go wrong. The original plan was that I would stay for about six weeks and that we would then fly to Costa Rica together to meet William and my mother. It was going to be a big family reunion, the one we'd all been waiting for.

I paid Cory's fare in advance and he seemed very excited about the trip. When I got to the States, however, he seemed to change. I began to feel he'd put on a front during his stay in England, and that now I was seeing the 'real' him. He started to put things off and mess me around. First, he said he couldn't actually afford any accommodation in Costa Rica, so couldn't go with me. I was annoyed he hadn't told me before as we could have changed our plans. From then on, he kept changing his mind as to whether he was going or not. In the end, I decided to cancel my flight and I came back home after only three weeks. I was pregnant with Samuel at the time, and had just got tired of all the indecision. I told Cory that he could go by himself if he wanted.

Not long after, he did. Although I was pleased for my mother and William that they would meet him, I was very disappointed. I'd dreamt of us all being together as a family again and suddenly, they had all met up without me. I don't have very much faith in Cory now. He's really let me down and I've lost trust in him. He's upset me greatly. I feel much closer to William.

My main aim now is to try and get my mother and William over here so they can see Samuel and get some idea of my life in England. It may be an impossible dream and arranging the trip will be very complicated and expensive, especially with William in a wheelchair. But I'm determined to try. I'm very glad I've done what I've done and met them. I feel much more complete. I'm glad for Samuel too, as I also want him to know about his roots and background.

Nicky

If another adoptee came to me right now and asked whether they should search for their birth parents, I'd tell them to do it, but think very seriously about the consequences. It can stir up emotions and feelings which are hard to anticipate.

I remember my childhood as good. I knew from an early age that I was adopted and I felt more special than everyone else around me. I can remember the day Mum told me. I was in the greenhouse with her and she told me I had two birthdays: one when I was actually born and the second when she and Dad brought me home. She told me I was special and that I was wanted more than most other children because they'd found me, wanted to keep me, and loved me. I was only five when she told me all this, so I didn't really understand. But the word 'special' stuck in my head. I used to get a birthday card on my actual birthday and a special card on my second 'birthday' too.

I began to feel different from other children when I started school. I realised that they looked like their parents, yet I didn't look like mine. I was also in and out of hospital a lot, which increased these feelings. In my early teens, I suffered from anorexia and ME. I had counselling about my anorexia and I think some of it was put down to my being insecure. At the time, I was starting to understand properly what being adopted meant.

Mum and Dad were always very open when I asked about my birth mother. They told me her name (Nina), where she came from, what her job was and that I had been born in the same area as the one we lived in. Nina had been twenty-two when she had me, but after my birth, she had moved to Wales.

One day, Mum got all my adoption papers out and showed them to me. It was as if all the details were about a different person: not me. They had this other name on them – Sarah – which I couldn't relate to at all. At the time, it was impossible for me to grasp that I'd actually come from another person.

As time went on, I started to think more deeply about it and things really began to sink in. I noticed little things about my family that were different from me. I don't know whether this was because I knew I was adopted, so I put a barrier up, or whether it was simply a teenage rebellion on my part. We argued like any other family would and I would occasionally round on them during rows and say I was going to run away and find my real parents. That must have killed them. Although my mum and I were very close, I couldn't help wondering what it was like to have the genetic, biological tie that my friends had with their mothers. Even though I had a younger brother who was adopted, I never properly discussed the subject with him. We argued quite a lot and we didn't talk about it until he was about nineteen. I know he will never set out to trace his birth parents.

Once I fully understood that Mum and Dad were not my birth parents, I wanted to know who was. By my late teens, I'd got to the point of looking closely at everyone I met or passed in the street: did they have the same nose, eyes or hair as me? Could they be related? When I reached eighteen, I was quite focused on finding out more about myself.

I had lots of ideas about what my birth parents would be like. My main thoughts were concentrated on my mother: it was important that I found out what she looked like and discovered all the little details about her that make up a person. I never considered actually building a relationship with her: I had my mum and never wanted to replace her. I just wanted to find the person who had given birth to me and understand more about why I had been given up. Finding my natural father never really came into the equation. Even though I knew he'd been around when I was born, I'd assumed that he and my mother had eventually gone their separate ways.

Once I was eighteen, I took a step forward. I had a very good male friend who really helped me. We went to the local town hall, got my birth certificate and approached NORCAP (see Appendix). For some reason, I didn't receive the information, and I didn't follow it through. Other things were happening in my life.

It was when I gave birth to my daughter, Poppy, that I finally decided the time was right. I was twenty-two. It was uncanny that I'd had my first daughter at the same age my mother had had me. Even more strangely, Poppy also weighed the same as I had: 6lb 2oz. And like my mother, I wasn't married, although I was in a stable relationship with Poppy's father, Mark.

I remember looking at Poppy when she was still only a few days old and wondering how anyone could possibly experience all the bonding through the pregnancy and all the pain, happiness and closeness of birth and then be able give the baby away. I thought that if my mother had gone through all that, she must have been some person.

I telephoned NORCAP again, joined up, and was assigned a counsellor. I found out that my natural parents had actually got married after my adoption, and that I had a full brother, whom they'd kept. It was a shock. At first, I felt happy they were together, because it made my search easier; but after a while, I felt confused. I couldn't understand why they had been forced to give me up if they could get married and have another child only four years later. Amongst all the information I had, there was a short statement from my mother saying that, at the time, she simply wasn't able to look after me. That was it. Very brief.

The details included an address where my mother had lived during her pregnancy. I remember driving up to the house and sitting outside in the car, just looking. I knew she wasn't there anymore, but I thought someone might know where she was. Yet I didn't even get out of the car to ask. I just sat there, staring.

NORCAP also gave me my father's parents' address, and his surname. Luckily, it was quite an unusual name, so I looked it up in the 'phone book for the area and there was only one listing. It had the right initial, so I rang the number. A man answered and I hung up. I did the same thing and hung up again. I was too scared to speak.

A friend and I then drove up to the address shown in the 'phone book. When we got there, we couldn't find the right road, so we stopped at a garage to check the way. My friend went in and asked where the road was. There was a young guy behind the counter and he laughed when she mentioned the road name. He asked her why she wanted to know and she made the excuse that we were meeting a friend there. He asked her what number house we wanted. I'd told her not say a number, so she skirted over it. 'I'm only asking because I live on that road,' he said.

The next thing I remember is her running out to the car saying, 'That guy in there looks just like you. He's the spitting image.' It was amazing. It clicked that he might be my brother.

I felt nervous, excited, sick. I also felt deceitful and guilty about sneaking around the way we were. We then drove to the road, had a look at the houses, but didn't do anything else.

Things happened quickly from there. NORCAP sent a 'cover' letter to the address saying they had a relative who wanted to get in contact. The wait was dreadful. I sat by the telephone a lot of the time. I was terrified of being rejected. I had to wait three weeks in the end, which was awful, as I thought the length of time was bound to mean bad news. Finally, NORCAP rang and told me my father, John, had been in contact. Shock hit me. I'd assumed that Nina would ring first and I was confused as to why it hadn't been her. But John had said he wanted to call me.

From then on, every time the 'phone went, my heart stopped. Whenever I answered it and it was someone else, it was a huge relief. A couple of days later he rang. My first thought was 'Help!' He had a strange, country accent. Almost instantly though, I felt I'd found the missing link. My identity was complete because, suddenly, I knew they were there, I knew they were real. We spoke for about half an hour. He was over the moon and said he couldn't wait to meet me. After about five minutes, we started to talk about what had happened regarding my adoption and afterwards – although not in detail. I told him about my life, and he told me about theirs. I found out that I didn't just have one brother, but another brother as well, which again, was a shock. John was very keen to arrange a meeting. This took me aback a little, as NORCAP had told me it might be a good idea to strike up a correspondence first. My initial reaction was therefore, 'Hang on a minute.' But then I decided that writing would prolong the agony for all of us. So I just thought, 'No, let's do it,' and agreed to the idea.

When I put the 'phone down, I burst into floods of tears. I was completely fraught. All the emotions that had built up in me for so long were suddenly released. Up until that point, it had all been a dream and I had feared the worst. Now it had actually happened and it was good news! I was surprised at how excited John had been, as I'd expected him to be very calm and cool. The one thing that worried me was that he hadn't really spoken about Nina's reaction. He and I had agreed to meet at some point soon, but she didn't seem to be in the picture at all.

Over the next couple of days, I spoke to John a few more times. During the last call, I asked him to ask Nina whether she wanted to speak to me. I knew the situation might be a bit delicate, so I wanted to give her the choice. She came on the 'phone. I remember our conversation well, because it was just full of laughter. Whether it was just nervous laughter I don't know, but we got on fine.

The three of us arranged to meet the next Sunday, which just happened to be Mother's Day. I found out later why Nina had put off talking to me. The NORCAP letter had been a huge jolt for her and had brought back a lot of painful memories which she was trying to deal with. I think she'd put a lid on the past, and now had to lift it up again.

About ten days before the meeting, I knew I had to tell my adoptive mum and dad. I hadn't told them anything before, as I'd wanted to know the outcome of my search before possibly hurting them unnecessarily. Now I knew I had to say something, as I couldn't go ahead with a meeting behind their backs.

Mum and Dad came round to my house. I sat them down and explained that I'd wanted to find the missing link in my life and that John and I had spoken. I reassured them that I didn't want to replace them, but just wanted to find out who my natural parents were. Dad was very quiet and Mum seemed quite excited. I was relieved that they knew, but I was worried for them.

The next week, however, proved quite difficult. There was less contact between us, and when I went round to their house, I felt a little uncomfortable. The news was beginning to sink in and Mum seemed less happy about the meeting.

Mother's Day came. I went to see Mum beforehand to give her a card and present. As the time for me to leave drew closer, the tension started to build. Dad put his arm round me and told me not to worry. I remember that vividly. As always, they were being very loving and caring, and I was worried about upsetting them. I was building myself up into a frantic state, to the point where I thought I couldn't go through with the meeting. I got upset and ran up to the bathroom in tears. My brother followed me and told me I had to go through with what I'd started. I'd arranged to meet John and Nina at a local hotel. I arrived five minutes early. I was shaking like a leaf and crying. I kept telling myself to calm down. I waited at reception for fifteen minutes, in pure torture.

Suddenly, there was a tap on my shoulder and a hand turned me round. She was hugging me and we both burst into tears. I can still hear the echo of myself crying. I hadn't seen her face and we stood there, holding each other for about three minutes. She wouldn't let me go and we kept telling each other we couldn't look up because our mascara would have run. Eventually, we pulled away and had a good look at each other. I had been told she was blonde, but she wasn't. I expected her to be the spitting image of me, but I could only see a vague similarity. John had stepped back a bit, but then he came over and gave me a big hug. I couldn't see any resemblance between him and me at all. The most amazing thing was that Nina was dressed in virtually the same outfit as me. We were both wearing kilts, with polo neck jumpers and thick black tights.

We went into the hotel bar and spent the next three hours talking and looking at photos. The conversation was very easy and comfortable. They talked a little about why they'd given me away. They told me that they couldn't afford to keep me at the time, but didn't go into much more detail. I wanted to know more, but didn't push it any further.

Apart from that, there were lots of laughs and it all felt very natural. I discovered Nina's sense of humour was just like mine: warped. That was nice. I felt I'd done the right thing in arranging the meeting, although I did feel guilty about Mum and Dad. It also became very clear that Nina and John wanted to build a relationship with me, that our meeting was never going to be a one-off.

When it came to the end, I didn't want to let them go. After twenty-five years, three hours wasn't long enough. When we parted, Nina cuddled me and we cried again. It was very emotional and we arranged to meet again the next day.

That afternoon, I went to see Mum and Dad. I was in shock I guess, and I wanted to tell them all about it, but knew I had to play it down. I just wanted to tell them how it had gone, but I found it difficult. I must admit that when I got there, it hit me fully that they weren't my natural, biological parents. But in my head, I knew they were and always would be my mum and dad.

Poppy, my partner Mark and I went to Nina's and John's house the day after. My brothers, Simon and Paul, were in the kitchen. I just walked in and said 'hello'. They just said 'hi' back. We didn't hug. It was quite distant. It was weird, because they felt like complete strangers, whereas Nina and John hadn't. Perhaps it was because I didn't know much about them: I'd got a lot of information about Nina and John, but not about them. They had also only been told about me a week before. Apparently, they'd thought that Nina was joking when she told them and they'd had far less time than me to get used to the idea of having an elder, full sister. Later that day, when we all went for a walk, Simon told me I was a 'nice shock', and explained that he'd always been the elder and wasn't anymore. I don't know whether he was saying it in a jokey way or whether he was hurt.

After that day, I started to wonder whether I'd done the right thing and how events were going to unfold. I wanted to carry on seeing them all, but on my terms. I hadn't gone into the reunion wanting a replacement family, but it was evident that they wanted a lot from me. After a few weeks, I didn't know whether to say that I didn't want permanent, frequent contact or whether to leave things to see how they developed.

That was six months ago, and I've left things. I've now met most of Nina's family and we see each other regularly, at least once a month, going out for meals and drinks. They 'phone me every week, but I call them very rarely – I don't need to!

A few weeks ago, Mark, Poppy and I went on holiday with John, Nina and the boys for a week in Cornwall. Initially, I wasn't sure about going, but we decided we needed a break. We thought that even if it turned out to be a disaster, at least we could simply get back in the car and drive home.

When we got there, I knew immediately it was going to be difficult as we had just two rooms in a small hotel. Over the course of the week, I began to realise that Nina had quite an overwhelming personality. She was bubbly and energetic all of the time. She also kept calling me Sarah instead of Nicky.

She'd done that right from the start, but I'd reassured myself that it was understandable and that she would stop after a while. However, she continued, and worst of all, she called me Sarah in front of Poppy, several times. One morning, she told me that Poppy had referred to me as 'Mummy Sarah'. I was furious, but I kept my anger inside. I just said, 'Oh. Mum will be pleased with that.' Nina replied, 'Well, you'll always be Sarah to me. You were my baby and that's what you were named.'

Because I've got Poppy, I could understand Nina's feelings, but I was upset that she hadn't been more sensitive about my position. She's very stubborn. As the week progressed, it became clear that John was calmer. Also, one day, I detected a slight atmosphere between Nina and myself that I couldn't quite identify. I don't know what it was: was I intruding between her and John? At the end of the week, although I'd had a good time, I was pleased to be able to go back home and have some space again.

It's now a few weeks since the holiday and I feel like I've opened up Pandora's box. Although I like being with Nina and John and we get on very well, I can't look at them and see them as my parents. When I fell over as a child, they weren't the ones to pick me up, they didn't bring me up. They weren't around, so I have no memories, no history with them. They are, effectively, two strangers, and it was just a case at the start of my finding out a little about them. The closest we'll ever be is good friends, but they'll never be part of me. I thought at the beginning that their excitement at meeting me would calm down after a while, but it hasn't really.

So right now, I feel like I'm stuck in the middle. The relationship I wanted to keep stable – my links with Mum and Dad – has changed slightly, as any relationship does when you go through things together. I now just want to stand up in front of everyone and shout, 'What about me?' From the start, I've always been the one who's had to apologise and explain. I think I've been expected to take everyone else's feelings into consideration and put them above my own. I feel as if I'm not allowed to make my own decisions.

Looking back, maybe if I'd never met Nina and John, maybe if I'd just had a photo of them, then I wouldn't be in this situation of balancing and juggling everyone's feelings and emotions. Nor would I feel guilty about Mum and Dad. But I can't, and don't, regret what I've done, simply because I had to do it.

Jon

I was born in London in 1959 and adopted in Liverpool in the same year, aged only three weeks. I was adopted by a Jewish family on the understanding that I had been born of a Jewish father.

My first home was a working-class Jewish home in Toxteth, Liverpool. The district was tough. My adoptive dad was a factory worker, my adoptive mum was a housewife: she'd given up her career when she got married. My father's brother – my uncle – lived in the small, two-up, two-down house with us, so it was pretty cramped. I was lucky in that I was sent to the local Jewish school in the posh part of town, so I got a good education. If I'd gone to the local school, I'd probably be working in a factory right now.

Mum and Dad were actually in their late forties when they adopted me but they lied about their age to the courts, saying they were in their early forties. They were desperate to have a child. As far as I'm aware now, Mum had suffered a number of miscarriages and had been advised she could never have children.

They didn't adopt any other children, so as I grew up, there were four of us in the house. The issue of my adoption was dealt with when I was still very small. They told me the story of where I came from in terms of my being 'special' and 'chosen' – the social worker's standard patter. The other option was to say, 'You're just an unwanted bastard,' so I guess they had no choice.

So, I grew up with three people who were, basically, pensioners. It was a pretty difficult time, especially as I reached my teens. I felt extremely isolated and as if I was living in a museum. I also harboured a strong sense of being 'out of place' in Liverpool. It was as if the city was a strange planet: I couldn't understand the mentality of the people. I just went along with it, especially when I was younger, since I was keen to be an ordinary 'scouser'. But as I got older, I rejected the world of football, drink and violence that was around me. I wanted to listen to Bach and go to the opera and I didn't like the Beatles who were then all the rage.

Mum and Dad were also extremely protective towards me. When I started to do the adolescence thing, they tried to tie more and more ropes around me, which I found very frustrating. The last summer I spent at home before I went to university proved to be highly problematic. For three months, there was practically a state of war in the house. I constantly battled against them in the hope that I would be given some respect and that they would accept that I was grown-up and wanted to spend time with my friends. It wasn't as if I was hanging out doing evil things: we weren't doing drugs or having sex or anything. I just wanted a modicum of freedom.

The result was an entire summer of fighting. How much of it was due to dissimilar natures or just my own 'teen rebellion', I'll never be able to quantify. But I know now there was a fundamental misunderstanding between us all. I think Mum was always looking to find out who I was like in the family and I believe she deluded herself in some ways that I would somehow become one of them. The more she tried to pin my character down, the more I raged against it.

All along, I knew there was something not quite right with my life. Something was missing that I just couldn't put my finger on. I could rationalise that my mum and dad weren't my real parents. There was a tangible distance between us, as if a slight shutter was up. When they started to get heavy about what I was allowed to do, I'd simply block it out and say to myself, 'They're not my real parents, so I'm entitled to not do what they want me to do.' I also used to reassure myself that I would find my natural parents one day. I fantasised about my real mother and father: what they might look like, what they might be like, what we might talk about. It was my retreat, as if I was saying, 'I don't like the ones I've got, so I'll fantasise about my other, proper ones.' Unusually, it was my father rather than my mother who was the most dominant issue for me. I don't know why. Finding my mother was a stepping stone to finding him. He was my target and my goal, right from the beginning.

When I reached eighteen, I knew it would be possible for me to start searching. But I decided not to do anything then, and to wait until my adoptive parents died. I had compassion for them and I was also scared of the implications of my search – I didn't know what I was going to find. I also had very little to go on. Mum and Dad never told me anything about my background, so I knew no details. So I left everything, thinking that maybe, one day, I'd start to trace.

My urge to get away from home was much stronger than anything else at this point. My priority was to get as far away from Liverpool as possible, so I chose prospective university courses which were not available in my 'home' city, just to make sure I didn't end up there. I was interested in psychology, but I chose philosophy to ensure I escaped. I ended up at Hull, but hated it. I did my essays, got decent results, and got very involved in Zionist politics. However, it was a dull place and I eventually gave up the course.

The previous year, I had been offered a place at Leeds University to read Arabic and Hebrew, but had decided I wasn't interested. I now changed my mind and headed for Leeds. Before my course began, I started to brush up on my Arabic. It was at this point that I finally found myself completely free and alone. I hadn't made any new friends at that juncture and it was a good moment to do something intensely private: to find out about me.

I approached Leeds Social Services and obtained my original birth certificate, which gave me my original birth name – Jonathan Bradley. It told me that my birth mother was British and a teacher, and that my father was a Syrian Jew and that they'd probably met at university. There was a whole little story written down. However, there was a blank where my father's name should have been. My immediate feelings were similar to those you have when you've just had a great meal: I felt, 'Fantastic! I know who I am now – I'm part Syrian and my mother's not Jewish.' It was as if I had another escape from the identity that had been given to me. I had a get-out. I accepted what I found and didn't do anything else. I knew enough and I let it go.

I'd kept the news of my search secret from Mum and Dad, because I wanted to see what the outcome was before I told them anything. I also felt very private about it, because it was very personal to me.

However, not long afterwards, Dad came to visit me in Leeds. I left him in my room while I went to make a cup of tea and when I came back, I realised he'd been looking through my cabinets. He'd found my birth certificate and confronted me with it. He gave a little speech about how he and Mum would be willing to help me find out what I needed to know. I didn't know whether I could trust him or not, but the fact was that at that stage, I wasn't on a mission. I had no sense of urgency. I'd done what I wanted to do and was satisfied. I didn't want all the tears and arguments that might start if I continued, as I knew Mum would take it as a rejection.

I settled in Leeds, got involved in the whole college scene and continued my life without doing anything further until 1986. I was happy to leave things alone. After leaving university, I threw myself into work and got involved in music. I ended up managing a jazz band and touring Europe constantly. It was much more attractive to me at the time than what I viewed as 'chasing my shadow', grabbing at it and asking 'Right, who are you?'

By the mid-1980s, the jazz thing had collapsed. I didn't want to get involved in music again and I returned to Liverpool. Once there, I asked Dad about my real father. He came over to me in a sort of huddle, and said, 'Well, son, he was an Israeli. He was in the Israeli army, he had problems, and he had to go back there to do military service. He had an influential uncle in Manchester. That's all I know.'

I presumed he was telling me the truth and thought, 'Hey, this is interesting.' (By this time, I had completely turned away from Zionism and had become very pro-Palestinian.) My first thought was that I had to go to Israel and see what it was like. I arranged my trip through the Israeli immigration service – I simply told them I had an Israeli father – and they were very accommodating.

A couple of months later, I was in Tel Aviv working as an English teacher. The city itself was a young, lively place, with lots of sunshine and beaches. It was fun at first. However, during my year there, my skin became very, very dark because of the sun. Increasingly, Palestinians would start to come up to me in the street and talk to me in Arabic, assuming I was one of them. Unfortunately, Israelis also started to think the same, which was not nice. It got the point where whenever I was out, I was getting pushed around, getting rifle butts in the side of me and was generally getting to be treated like a second-class citizen. Eventually, there was a knock on my door and I was deported. It was no problem. I wanted to go.

By this time it was 1987 and after a couple of weeks in Liverpool, I moved back to Leeds. I dedicated the next year to finding my birth parents. I got myself a job in a night club, in order to free up the daytimes for my search.

I knew I was searching for a Syrian father and a British mother. The tracing process was pretty easy and unremarkable. Basically, I ended up searching for every Bradley in the Yorkshire 'phone books and got lucky quite quickly. I contacted a cousin of my birth mother's who gave me her 'phone number and address in London.

I immediately called her, using a rather feeble cover story. She saw through it easily and we had a very brief conversation. We then exchanged letters. In mine, I talked about my trip to the Middle East and she wrote back saying that it was all very coincidental, as my father's home was in Kuwait. Loud bells clanged in my mind. In a few seconds, it felt like my whole life had been turned upside down. It just didn't make sense. I was a Jewish kid from Liverpool and I'd often been called 'typically Jewish'. Yet now it was dawning on me that my real father could not be a Jew. He must be Moslem. All the information I'd been given about him was total garbage.

A couple of weeks later, I met my mother and had a good old chin-wag. I realised then that it wasn't simply a question of asking her who my father was and then hailing her goodbye. I suppose that before, I'd had this notion that a woman who gives her child away does so maliciously and I guess I was quite angry with her in a way. I had just thought 'Why?' (I learnt later, through meetings with other birth mothers, that when a woman gives a child away, it was not a question of her not wanting the baby, and I began to understand the trauma involved in it.)

Yet when I met her, I thought, 'Hey, here's a relationship I've never had or really thought about.' Although we never really broached the subject of what she'd gone through in giving me up – she had an emotional closedness about her that seemed to prevent her from talking about it – we developed a terrific relationship. We maintained a long correspondence in the year following our first meeting and met up three or four times in that period. The similarities between us turned out to be quite profound. Our interests and our political opinions almost mirrored each other. I also sensed an energy between us that could not simply be explained by a mother–son relationship. There were strong, passionate undercurrents, almost like an affair, yet never anything physical. She sent me poems with all sorts of hidden meanings. I think she was re-living her relationship with my father through me. When we were out together, she'd walk along beside me, with this wonderfully proud look on her face. We made quite a distinctive couple because she's blonde and blue-eyed and I'm very dark. Everyone would look at us.

She had to tell her husband, Charles, who ironically, was also Jewish, about me, and also break the news to their two children, my two half-brothers. The younger one is called Jonathan, like me, and I was impressed that she'd managed to close her mind off from the name by giving it to her third child. Jonathan was eighteen and doing his A-levels at the time and he thought it was all great. The older half-brother, David, as far as I know, still doesn't know about me.

After a time, it became clear that there were problems between her and Charles over me. She had suddenly found this new relationship which she hadn't opened up about before and he was discovering the fact that she was besotted with me. There was a further complication in that, having married a Jewish man, she had converted to the Jewish faith. So, not only did he have to accept that his wife had had a child before their marriage which she had not told him about, he also had to face the fact that she'd had a relationship with an Arab, and now had an Arab son. She had created an interesting dilemma: one Arab son, two Jewish!

Obviously, I was still very keen to meet my birth father and my mother agreed to help me. All I knew was his name and that he was in Kuwait. In the end, the tracing took about six months. The key was an advert in *The Guardian* for a teaching post in Kuwait. My mother cut it out and sent it to me with the view that I should head out there and get work.

I 'phoned the number given, which was in Leeds. The woman who answered told me the vacancy was in a girls' school, so men couldn't apply. I put the 'phone down and thought, 'Hey, Kuwait's a small place, why don't I ask?' I called her back and asked if she happened to know my father. 'Yes of course, I know him!' she replied, 'My husband has worked for him for thirteen years!' She told me my father was a senior executive with an oil company and that he was a lovely man. She then gave me his 'phone number – there and then!

I telephoned him the next day and said, 'Hi, my name's Jonathan.' He'd been expecting to get a call from me at some point in his life, so he knew who I was immediately. He just said, 'Where are you?' and 'phoned me back within half an hour. (My mother had told him about me a few months after my birth and adoption, when he had come back to England for a visit. He'd been upset about what she had done.) He was very formal and although he spoke excellent English, the language barrier was evident. Despite his formality, I felt a definite warmth emanating from him. He told me was coming to London a few months later and we agreed to meet then. I put the 'phone down and felt pretty good. I'm sure I went out to celebrate.

We met up in the August of the same year at his flat in St John's Wood. I was still living in Leeds, but came down to London for the weekend. I got dressed up, jumped on my tatty Honda motorbike and drove over. It was a big, posh flat, overlooking the mosque at Regent's Park. A Filipino maid answered the door. My father's wife, who had known about me right from the start, wasn't far behind her, and rushed over to me in a great state of excitement. She gave me a big hug, saying, 'Come in, come in, eat, eat!'

My father was sitting in the lounge. He was very spruced up in a silk shirt, and was sitting very elegantly, but obviously very nervously in one of the armchairs. I walked into the room and saw a mirror in front of me – him. I looked into his face and it was mine. He was my absolute spitting image. Maybe a flatter nose, darker eyes and more jowly – but essentially an older version of me. (I remember thinking, that's where I get my hooter from!) It was instant recognition for both of us. Peas in a pod.

Our similarity was such that he instantly knew he wasn't a victim of a hoax. (From his point of view, it could have been anybody ringing up and introducing themselves as his long-lost son in order to get at his money). But our likenesses were so amazing, it was obvious I was his. We started to chat and develop the conversation. I can't remember what we talked about. But as time went on, I started to feel a great rapport with him. I found out he had two sons and a daughter, all in their mid-twenties, and that his daughter had a baby. They seemed to be just a happy bunch of rich people! He had worked in the oil business and had since moved into politics.

We met a few times over the next couple of years, before the Gulf War. Once, he mentioned to me that he was working very closely with his country's prime minister and I remember thinking, 'Is he telling me this because he wants me to back off?' It was just the tone which he used. He was confiding in me but also seemed to be hinting that I shouldn't get in the way or do anything which would jeopardise his position. I thought 'OK, fine.' It worried me a little.

However, whenever we did meet, there was this nice little 'twinkle' between us. I remember sitting in a hotel lobby with him once, and spending a few minutes looking at and commenting on the same women that went by. It was a sort of laddish, father–son thing that I'd never experienced before.

I got married the same year and he got into the habit of pushing money my way. He'd say, 'Go and take your wife out for a meal' and then hand me £200. There were very excited discussions about my going to Kuwait, but I recoiled from the idea. I think it was because of my experiences in the Middle East. I suppose I just needed more time to get used to the new 'me' I'd discovered. My self-image was going through a variety of changes and I needed space to absorb everything.

In 1989, I moved to Germany with my first wife, who was Czech-German, so she could find a job. The move was good in that it gave me the breathing space I needed. My father was in Kuwait most of the year and was coming to London every summer. As far as I was concerned, everything was good. Our relationship was left open, with no pressure from either side. It was nice and easy-going. It was good knowing he was there for me if I needed him. But there was also a bit of a barrier: our different cultures were a hindrance.

There was no such hindrance with my mother. We came from the same liberal, intellectual mould and have become really good buddies. About a year or so ago, we had a bit of a cooling-off period, mainly because Charles still gets very tense about us meeting. Apparently, he sulks the day after we meet up, but they have a good marriage and I understand that she has to put that first.

Up until the Gulf War, the relations between myself and my father were fine. Since then though, things have changed. When the war started, everyone went into complete craziness and panic. Through an instance of clumsiness on my part, my father's colleagues and friends got to know who I was and who my father was. He was extremely upset and effectively shut the door on me. I apologised several times for my blunder, which I accept was nothing less than a blunder. He had given me financial support for some time, which had cushioned me over a number of years. He withdrew that, without notice, around a year ago, and I haven't heard a word from him since. I wonder now whether my clumsiness was an excuse for him to get me off his back. He may have been looking for a way out anyway, I don't know. So, all my searching, all my hard work to find him, all that fantastic enthusiasm, all those good vibes between us have been reduced to virtually nothing. If I could change things – erase the mistake I made – I would in an instant. But it seems that I can't.

The situation is now back to square one. I haven't met my two half-brothers or my half-sister. I feel blue. It's just difficult to live with. My first marriage ended and I've now re-married. My wife and I are proud parents of a nineteen-month-old baby girl and I wonder what I'm going to tell her when she starts asking about her grandparents and background. It's going to be really hard: telling her about her grandfather in Kuwait. I've sent him pictures of her and written to him several times – but I got no response.

One good thing that has happened is that I've now 'come out' as an Arab and become part of the Arab community in London. Most of them know my father and there are people in the network who might agree to having a 'word in his ear' on my behalf.

Despite the situation, I don't regret tracing my birth parents at all. Finding and meeting them was a necessary part of my development. Often when adoptees go through reunions, especially if they have an emotional insecurity, they need to create a notion of a 'father and mother' out of two strangers. It's very difficult to do, but it's very hard to avoid doing: because that's what the two strangers are. Whether an adoptee is successful or not in doing this depends on the personality and circumstances involved.

There are definitely still wounds that I feel because I'm adopted. The best way to describe it is to say that there are parts of me which remain hidden and inaccessible. I can't get into them. I don't know whether I ever will.

Julia

I was handed over to my adoptive parents when I was about six weeks old, after presumably having been with my natural mother until then. This all happened back in 1957.

I knew all along that I was adopted. I wasn't told on a specific occasion, it was just talked about from a very early age. I also had an adopted brother, so my parents would have had to have told us both.

My parents were probably what could be described as working class. Dad managed a grocery store and Mum did menial jobs such as cleaning and other work. They were both in their late thirties when I was adopted and believed, at that time, that Mum couldn't have children. It's an irony that much later on, some of her old medical records turned up showing that she had been pregnant earlier in life and that she had undergone a termination without her knowledge. I don't know any more details, but I know they were both upset when they found this out.

I remember growing up and feeling that being adopted was just the normal run of things. It seemed normal because my brother and I were conditioned to believe it was and because Mum and Dad both 'went by the book' when it came to explaining our background. They followed the accepted philosophy of the time, telling us that we were very special because we had been 'chosen'.

I didn't really have a problem with being adopted at school. The only occasion I can remember the subject arising was when I was at secondary school and an older boy asked why my brother 'looked like a wog'. My brother is half-Iranian so he looks Middle Eastern. I also had a close girlfriend and I remember being vaguely envious of her relationship with her mother. I didn't know exactly what it was I was jealous of, but it was certainly there. I was also envious of other people's family homes – and other, seemingly normal families: I felt they were different from ours.

Generally, I can't say I had a happy childhood. I had moments of happiness, but my mum had personality problems that made it difficult for her to accept me and my brother for what we were. She had an obsession with illness and was very prying, and we weren't allowed to be 'kids'. If we played up, she would get extremely annoyed and stressed. She was also neurotic, which meant she'd be forever fussing over little things. She was constantly looking into what I was doing and yet she wasn't maternal at all. She was physically cold and distant and we have never been close.

I was much closer to my adoptive dad. He was a very open man, and I believe he related to me because his own mother had not wanted him. (In fact, as a boy, he had been given to his grandmother to be looked after.)

The knowledge that I was adopted was interwoven with a strong curiosity to know who my birth mother was. As I approached adolescence, this curiosity became insatiable and I had recurring dreams about her. I knew there was a foreign element in my history, so I used to fantasise about her being from another country. I assumed she was probably from a higher-class background than my parents and used to dream she was walking past me in the street. This mirrored reality: I used to study people's faces all the time, searching for someone that looked like me, some little sign.

I definitely missed a sense of continuity and of knowing my place in the world. Everything seemed so airy-fairy. Mum and Dad had told me that I had been chosen, but that in itself didn't answer any questions. I looked very different from them and was constantly questioning why I behaved in a different way; why I had particular tastes and talents that no one else in the family had. My sense of identity was extremely weak.

At school, everyone had high hopes for me and I was regularly told I was good enough to go to university. But I remember deciding that I would sabotage everyone's ambitions for me, starting with my eleven-plus. I sat down to the exam and deliberately put down all the wrong answers, basically to put a bomb under my own achievements. I did this type of thing right through childhood: to 'get' at 'them'. With Mum, this manifested itself in my saying some really wicked things. When I was seventeen, just before I left home, I told her, 'I'm never going to have a white wedding that you can come to.'

Looking back, I can see that I was very, very angry. I think it all tied in with my first two or three months of life. It was my anger that, as a baby, I had been foisted on to this stranger who had then proceeded to change me and touch me. I believe it's left me with difficulties when it comes to physical touching. I have problems getting close to people. The need to sabotage myself and other people's hopes and plans for me has also stayed with me.

By the time I was thirteen or so, I was getting involved with a bad crowd at school. I ended up going to court and having to see a probation officer every two weeks for two years. It turned out to the best thing that ever happened. I remember her as being very, very good with me and very interested in the fact I was adopted. She encouraged me to talk about my adoption with her, which was a huge relief. Suddenly, here was someone I could open up to who knew some of the psychological issues involved. I told her about the problems I was encountering at home and everything I felt. It's only in retrospect that I can see how she was connecting my situation with my being adopted. I didn't fully realise it at the time.

In April 1975, the new Adoption Law came into effect, which allowed adoptees to search actively for their mothers. It was good timing for me because 1975 was the year I became eighteen. I remember reading about the change in the law in the papers and thinking 'Yes, yes, yes.' I was itching to do something. I had a burning desire to find my 'real' mother.

By this time, I had left home and was living on the road as a traveller. It was the end of the hippy era and I guess I was doing some rebelling. I ended up living in Bristol and eventually settled down with a job. I sent for my adoption papers and went through them with a social worker. They didn't tell me much, but I found my mother's address on my original birth certificate. She had been living in London.

I decided to move there and got myself a live-in mother's help job in Battersea. Once there, I contacted the adoption agency who had overseen my case and they invited me for an interview. I remember it as if it was yesterday. I walked into a room and there, behind a huge desk, was an archetypal, blue-rinsed woman looking very intimidating. The room had this tangible air of fustiness. She looked at me and I could tell instantly she felt very bitterly about the change in the law. She seemed to hail from a different era where, after adoption, both adoptee and birth mother simply wipe the slate clean. I remember her saying, 'Well Miss Jones. You're a right little mongrel, aren't you?' She told me about my mother, whose name was Stella, and who was of Greek Cypriot extraction. She also told me my original name was Maria Mavromatis. She told me a few more details, but I couldn't help sensing that some of the information was wrong.

I came out of the interview and felt so depressed and degraded that I contemplated jumping into the Thames. I had been treated in a horrible way.

I suddenly had all this information about myself and my mother but I didn't know what to do next. I made a few forays to St Catherine's House, but encountered real problems in finding my mother's birth certificate. The information I found simply didn't make sense and I concluded I was tracing the wrong person. Because of this problem, I left the whole thing. I simply let it go. Looking back, I'm glad I did, because I think, in hindsight, that I wasn't really ready.

Four years later, I went back to St Catherine's to renew my search and solved the mystery. I had been tracing the right person after all: it was simply that my mother's birth had been re-registered at a date after her original birth. I went on to discover she had given birth to another baby girl – my half-sister, Jane, six years after me – and that she too had been adopted. She had then had another girl – my half-sister, Anna – a few years later and had married and had had two boys, Chris and Colin.

I remember feeling physically sick that she had put her second child up for adoption. I was very shocked and couldn't understand why she hadn't learnt from her mistakes. I started to wonder what sort of woman she was.

I can't remember exactly how it happened, but I then found somebody in London who actually remembered my mother living next door. I then found out my mother's address. It was amazing, because she lived in Kentish Town, practically just down the road from where I lived. It was startling. I felt physically sick when I heard how close she was to me.

Soon after, a couple of friends offered to help me make the first approach. They suggested they should come with me and talk to Stella about me without my being present. It seemed the best way to approach things and I trusted them implicitly.

On the day we'd planned, they drove me to my mother's address, left me in the car and knocked on the door. They'd devised a cover story which would allow her to 'read between the lines'. I was lying down on the car seat, my face in my hands, feeling terribly sick. I couldn't watch. The next thing I knew was that a woman was coming towards the car. She leaned into the open window, saw me and said, 'Ooh, you look just like Anna!' I felt like I was in a 'fight or flight' situation. My adrenaline was pumping, my ears were buzzing. It was as if I was watching a film about the reunion; not really involved, but observing myself and this woman from a distance. I was in shock I suppose.

My two friends melted away and I was left with Stella in the family house. I can't identify precisely what I felt that first afternoon. I remember thinking that I did look like her, although physically, she was shorter than I thought she would be. The way she used her hands while she talked was familiar and I spotted quite a few facial likenesses. But what was amazing was that in the sitting room, there were loads of owls – paintings of owls, owl statues and owl toys. It was strange, because I too had a fascination for owls.

I remember Stella crying throughout the meeting. (It's interesting that, after that, she never became emotional in front of me again.) She was very unsettled and shocked, and as a result, I suppose I didn't make the best use of my time with her. I asked about my father and she told me he was American. His name was Jerry, he'd been over in England to visit relatives in London and she'd met him at the Hippodrome Dance Hall. However, she couldn't meet him for their next date as she was ill and could never find him after that. The other revelation was that she had not told anyone – her husband, Michael, or her children – about me or my adopted sister, Jane. I asked her directly about Jane. To my amazement, she replied: 'Who's Jane?' I responded by saying, 'Jane Mavromatis, born 5 December 1963.' She realised I knew the truth and she had to explain what had happened. I stayed with Stella for a couple of hours or more, after which she told me that her children were due to arrive so I would have to leave.

A couple of days later, I received a frantic 'phone call from her. She was terribly uptight about what she should do and said she was thinking of telling Michael that I was her younger sister who had just turned up out of the blue. I didn't feel very comfortable about the idea, to say the least, but I didn't tell her how I felt. I decided it was up to her to tell Michael in whatever way she wanted. Eventually, she did tell him the truth and he seemed to be generally all right about it.

My boyfriend and I met Michael and Stella in a pub a few days later. The atmosphere was very odd and again, I felt I was watching a TV show about myself. It didn't seem real at all. Stella chatted a lot. I was beginning to realise how talkative and extrovert she was and that she had a very strong personality. My feelings towards her were very mixed. There was something about her and the whole situation that I couldn't quite grasp. I felt close to her in some respects, but I sensed there were hidden, darker sides to her.

I met Anna, my fifteen-year-old half-sister, around a week later. I was waiting at the family home and we were introduced. I noticed that she was very cowed and quiet in a strange sort of way. It wasn't the normal shyness or reticence that a teenager might show at meeting new people. She didn't seem to be extrovert like Stella at all, and all her responses to the conversation were on one level. I thought her behaviour was quite strange and I sensed she was unhappy.

By this stage, I was getting drawn into the family but was still keeping to myself to a large degree. Stella picked up on this and began to see me as something of a dark horse. Perhaps because of this, she asked me whether I planned to stay in contact with the family as she didn't want to tell Colin and Chris about me if I was not going to be around. She said they were at an impressionable age and that it would be hurtful and pointless to tell them unless I was going to be part of the long-term picture. I, of course, told her that I would like to stay in contact.

I was introduced to the two boys – who were only ten or eleven at the time – as their half-sister and also to Michael's family. I also started to make regular visits to the family home. The boys proved to be very easy and accepting about me, even fascinated by me. The youngest, Colin, couldn't understand why I didn't call Stella 'Mum'. The memory of this question has stayed with me until now, simply because I couldn't answer it satisfactorily. I suppose that it sums up the problem of missing years.

Only a few weeks after our first meeting I started to notice how controlling Stella was. She used to say 'This is my house, and in my house, what I say goes.' All the kids – Anna, Chris and Colin – were corralled into doing household chores on a regimental basis and she started to behave towards me in the same way. I was twenty-four at this stage and although part of me felt trapped, a stronger part of me was feeling very angry about it. I was being treated like a child and I harboured a deep resentment. I knew that it wasn't all to do with Stella's treatment of me. I was also keeping one of her secrets – the secret of Jane. She'd had a second child adopted and although she'd come clean about me, she hadn't told the whole truth. I found it increasingly difficult to keep Jane's existence quiet and, in fact, I ended up telling Anna.

All my resentment came out one night when Stella started to admonish me about my life. She accused me of being irresponsible: I was twenty-four, still unmarried, lived in a rented flat and wore hippie clothes. I was very hurt and angrily retorted that even though my life wasn't perfect, at least I wasn't going around dropping babies here there and everywhere. I remember I had been drinking at the time and I tend to come out with aggressive statements when I've had one too many. Naturally, my outburst didn't go down very well and from then on, Stella has been colder towards me. Things were never the same afterwards. There was a definite sense of my being 'frozen out'.

By this stage, it was becoming clear that my half-sister, Anna, was very unhappy. I started to joke with her that I would help if she wanted to move away from Stella and Michael. As it was a joke, I didn't expect her to take me up on the offer, so I was very surprised and shocked when she telephoned me at work one day and told me she had packed a suitcase and was ready to leave. I look back now and think encouraging her was the biggest mistake of my life. It went on to cause a huge rift within my birth family.

I ended up taking Anna to my adoptive parents. I'd told them that I'd met my birth family – I think I mumbled it over a cup of tea one afternoon – and they hadn't really said much about it from then on. We have never been good at communicating, although we got on quite well on a surface level. However, they were very generous in agreeing to let Anna stay. She moved in and settled down quite quickly.

Stella and Michael obviously wanted her back. I can't remember the exact chain of events, whether I implicated myself as the progenitor of it all or not. I think that in the end, I felt I had to tell them where she was, as Stella had told me that they'd informed the police.

The next thing that happened was that Stella and Michael turned up at my adoptive parents' house and forced Anna to leave. My mum didn't think much of Stella at all. Anna was in a state of shock and didn't want to go, but she was forced to.

That was the end of it. I haven't spoken to Stella in the thirteen years since. Neither of us has really tried to contact the other. I tried writing to her when I gave birth to my son, but she never replied. I suppose my letter may have been confrontational – I didn't mean it to be – but sometimes my brusque manner means I can come over that way.

Although I haven't seen or heard from Stella I had a visit from my younger brother recently. It was really good to see him again, but it was sad to hear from him that Stella hasn't changed at all. I have also tried to build a relationship with Anna again, and at one point three or four years ago, we met several times. However, I don't think she could handle it. I wanted her to ask Stella about my family history and it got to the point where she stopped answering my 'phone calls. More lies and deceit were at work maybe. I wrote her a letter but she never replied.

It's a very sad outcome. But I've since found out – through research into my family history – that there have been quite a number of deceptions and cover-ups in my family; starting with my birth grandmother and continuing with my mother. Basically, there are two generations of illegitimate children: my mother and that of her three daughters: me, Jane and Anna.

This said, I'd still like to have regular, uncomplicated contact with my birth family – just enough to keep in touch with news. I'm not sure whether it will ever happen. My partner, Roger, would like to meet Stella, and has been trying to persuade me to write another letter; but a more gentle one than the previous missive. Maybe I will. I'm trying to work myself up to it. I now know that birth mothers suffer tremendous trauma when they give up their child and I know Stella had no counselling. I know she's suffered hugely.

I'd also love to meet my other half-sister, Jane, but I don't even know whether she has made contact with, or met, Stella. I'd also like to meet my birth father too. They're both missing parts of my family.

David

I wish I hadn't been adopted. I think it's affected me negatively in many ways, although in some ways positively. I've always had feelings of rejection, low self-esteem and insecurity, as well as a sense that I've never been in the right place.

I never fitted in during my childhood – with my home town, with my brothers, or with my adoptive parents. I have always felt alone and because of that, I've learnt how to do things more for myself than perhaps I would have done otherwise.

I was born in Hammersmith and from there was taken back home by my natural mother for two or three days. I then went to a private foster home where I was put up for adoption. Several months later, my adoptive parents took me home.

My adoptive father was a builder, my adoptive mother a housewife. They were good, straight people, with a reputation for being very honest and hard-working. We lived in Luton and it was a pretty secure background.

They adopted me because my adoptive mum had had a stillborn baby a few years earlier and had been told she probably wouldn't be able to have any children. Nine months later however, she discovered she was pregnant. My younger brother, their first natural son, was born eighteen months after I arrived in the family, and then another boy was born six or seven years later.

I wasn't actually told I was adopted. I found it out from my friends at school when I was six. A group of neighbours, including my parents, had all moved to the same street together because they were all friends, so everyone knew each other's business. One of the children in my group must have heard their parents speaking about me and told me.

I remember being hurt by the news, but I didn't really believe it. I asked my mother what it was all about. She told me it was true and that they had chosen me, which sounded like they had picked me just as you would a stray dog at a rescue centre. The 'chosen' message never really washed with me.

From the time my first brother was born, I was sent away to spend all my school holidays with my adoptive grandparents in a town nearby. I felt quite out of everything. I missed out on the new baby and I started to reason that it was because I was adopted. Even though I was quite young, I realised I was being treated differently from my parent's natural children. The same pattern continued when my second brother was born.

The fact was that I didn't consider myself part of the family. I also felt 'picked on' at home. My mother and father always seemed to take my brothers' side when there were arguments. I was the one who was smacked and punished. My younger brother was totally obnoxious to me. I remember one day, he lay at the bottom of the stairs and claimed I'd pushed him down. He would also bite his own arm to draw blood and accuse me of doing it. It was not nice and I started to feel a real resentment towards my 'family'.

From the age of around eight, I wanted to leave home. I used to walk to the end of the road determined to run away and then realise I had nowhere to go. I always went back with my tail between my legs. In my teens, I used to confront my parents a lot, saying it was obvious that they didn't really love me. I just wanted out.

As soon as I knew I was adopted, I was curious about my birth mother. For a short time, I fantasised that my real parents were royalty and that I was a long-lost prince of some country somewhere. That phase passed pretty rapidly. From then on, I just told myself that whoever my birth mother was, a life with her was better than the life I had. It was a case of 'Well, if my adoptive family have a semi-detached house, then my real family will have a bigger, detached house, even a palace!' I built up this fantasy about my real family and I dreamt that one day, they would come and find me. They must have lost me by accident, somewhere in a crowd, and one day, they would rescue me, like in a fairy tale.

Despite my fantasies, I knew that I had to get on with my life, so between my teens and my late twenties, I put the whole idea of tracing my birth mother on the shelf. I was extremely wild – although quite successful career-wise – and travelling round a lot. My life was just too full to do anything at that stage.

Things changed when I was twenty-nine and my first son was born. I was living with my girlfriend in a small village near Bath. We'd decided to try the country life and settle down. The arrival of my own child brought the issue of my real parentage into sharper focus and I started to make enquiries about my birth parents.

My adoptive father died at around the same time, and one day, while I was back at my parents' home, I picked the combination lock on his briefcase to see what I could find. Inside, I found my adoption documents which told me my real parents' names (my mother was called Maggie), their ages, the fact that they had married after I was born and their reasons for having me adopted. The reason stated was simply 'lack of accommodation', which seemed strange to me at first, and then almost unbelievable. There were also transcriptions of two short interviews with my parents and I recall being very upset when I read that Maggie had been 'unusually and deeply distressed' about giving me away.

I then wrote to the Registrar General, and in the fullness of time, was passed on to a social worker who, presumably, was there to check that I was sane enough to find my real parents. After a number of counselling sessions with her and several months later, I was given my birth certificate and my parents' marriage certificate. A trip to St Catherine's House turned up nothing (I later discovered my mother was born in Scotland, so all my papers were in Edinburgh). I couldn't find my father's details either, which was, as I also discovered later, because he had been born in Argentina.

By this time, my personal life was getting complicated and my marriage was on hold, so I went to Tenerife to make a fresh start. Again, I left my search on the back burner. Over the next few years, I built up my own business which turned out to be very successful. Life was good and I had a villa, a speedboat, everything anyone could ever want. However, my marriage and family situation grew worse and to top it all, I became seriously ill with ME. The next few years were spent shuttling between the Canaries and England, spending all my money on medical bills. My life was going rapidly downhill.

On one of my trips back home, I went back to St Catherine's House and this time, found that I had a half-brother, who was eighteen months younger than me, and who had also been adopted. I felt disgusted that Maggie had been able to do the same thing twice. I started to search for my brother, but was told there was no way I could do it. I was then put in contact with a private social worker, who agreed to start a trace to find my birth mother.

Within four days, I received a 'phone call from the social worker saying she had found Maggie, who, apparently, was overjoyed and very keen to meet me. Taking the call was very difficult, as my adoptive mother was sitting in the room with me and I hadn't told her anything about my search. I had to hide my excitement and reverted to a 'Yes' and 'No' routine as the social worker told me the news. She told me Maggie was mailing photographs of herself that day and she asked me to go to London a few days later to see her and to talk. I was very fraught, but very excited too.

When I got to London on the day, the social worker told me what to expect from my reunion and informed me I had numerous brothers and sisters: six in fact. She then showed me the photos my mother had sent and gave me her telephone number. I couldn't see any similarities at all between me and Maggie. She was very small, barely five foot tall, nothing like me at all.

I got home, knowing I had to make the 'phone call. It took me some time to get myself together. I really had to steel myself to go through with it. Eventually, I picked up the 'phone and a woman answered. I just said, 'Hello?' Maggie took over from then on. 'Oh! Is that you David? Oh, this is fantastic!' I didn't get a chance to say much, she was so excited, she just gabbled. She asked me to go up to Ballater, in Scotland, where she was living.

I went up a few days later by coach. I was suffering from a bad bout of ME at the time, so was absolutely shattered and very fatigued. Consequently, I felt half-dead during the journey and didn't really get the chance to get all keyed up and concerned about what was about to happen. ME makes your mind go blank to a large extent, so maybe it was a blessing.

I was so weary that by the time the coach arrived at Aberdeen, it was a huge relief. As we pulled into the coach station, I peered out of the windows to see if I could spot Maggie, but I couldn't. However, as I came down the steps, I spotted a tiny woman in a black leather jacket leaping up and down. She recognised me instantaneously and ran across like a little dynamo and gave me several big hugs. She kept on leaping around and started to chatter uncontrollably. I couldn't get a word in edgeways and just stood there shell-shocked.

Maggie had brought a male friend with her who had a car, so we then all drove off to Ballater. I sat in the back and Maggie talked and talked. She went on and on, telling me about the aunts and family I was going to meet and saying how exciting the whole thing was. It was all washing over me as I felt so ill, but I got on well with her right from the start.

Our first port of call was to one of my aunts, Maggie's sister Carol, who had laid out a special tea for us. It turned out Carol was dying of cancer and was terribly pale and ill, but she was still very upbeat about seeing me. Carol's husband was there, and soon after, another of Maggie's sisters, Nan, turned up. Everybody was speaking in very broad Scottish accents, so I sometimes found it difficult to understand. We talked about everything but the past. The conversation was all about what my life was like, what I did in business and how great it was to see me. I tended to give very evasive answers as I didn't want them to know about my illness. They then started to talk about the family, and the photos came out. It felt like I was starting a new job and going into a strange office on my first day. I was being introduced to, and told about, lots of new people, but I didn't really know what was going on, and who was who.

The meeting confirmed that I did, indeed, have six half-siblings: Julia, who had been born before me and spent most of her life in children's homes; Georgie, my younger sister; Hazel and Alix, who were twins; and Tina and Gareth. Although I was told about them all – their names and ages anyway – I wasn't shown any photographs.

By this time, Carol was feeling ill, so Dennis (her husband) and I went to the pub. My mother and Carol eventually joined us, and a party started. The town was obviously a very close-knit community, and everyone in the pub seemed to know Maggie and that I was her son. Karaoke started, and I was introduced to what seemed like hundreds of people. I was getting drinks bought for me left, right and centre. Everyone insisted that Maggie and I should have a slow dance together, which we did, and they all went wild. The pub stayed open, and we celebrated until about five in the morning. At one point, Maggie clambered on to the pool table and danced on it. She's an extremely lively character, very bubbly. Even though I was feeling absolutely shattered, I was tremendously buoyed up by the excitement and elation around me.

That night I stayed at Maggie's house, which was very basic. I slept on the sofa and remember feeling disappointed that I'd met her at a time when I wasn't financially secure enough to help her. A few years earlier and I could have treated her to holidays and everything.

The next day we walked into town, where we seemed to meet most of the populace. Maggie knew everyone's names and they all seemed to know her and about me. We then went back to Carol's where I met my great aunt Meg, and then went back home.

While we were there, the 'phone rang. It was Hazel, one of my half-sisters. I remember hearing Maggie say to her: 'Oh!

You should speak to someone who's here with me – your brother!' She had never told Hazel about me. The 'phone was handed to me and there was Hazel, totally shocked. 'What's all this about?' she asked. I told her. Then she said, laughing, 'Is that it? Are there any more of you lurking around?' I replied, 'I don't know, there might be. You'd better ask Maggie!' The conversation was very stilted: she was pleasant, but completely taken aback. After that, the 'phone didn't stop. It was more of my sisters calling because they'd found out they had another brother.

I left Scotland the next day. Just before I did, Maggie gave me a tatty, rolled-up pile of papers, covered in scrawly handwriting. She explained that she'd written her life story and that she wanted me to read it. I waded through the papers on the coach journey home. She'd had an extremely tough life and I remember feeling very proud that she'd actually managed to hold things together. It turned out that Julia, her first child, was the product of a rape. After Julia was put into a children's home, Maggie had met and married my father: an aircraft engineer who was considerably older than her. He was attracted to her youth, but he wasn't interested in having children. The outcome was that when I was born, they fostered me out temporarily while they looked for a bigger home where we could all live. While Maggie was looking, she found out that my father had secretly put me up for adoption. She immediately rushed around to look for a home to try and get me back, but failed, and my adoption went ahead. The story tallied with her being so distressed at having to give me up, and with the reason for the adoption stated on my papers: 'lack of accommodation.' After that, Maggie and my father had eventually divorced, and Maggie had re-married twice – my other half-siblings being the end result.

Having read through her story, I realised she'd been one of life's victims and had been treated miserably by the men in her life. I felt a lot of sympathy for her, even though I knew it was only one side of the story and that my father might tell me a different one. However, I also found out that my father had died, alone, and without ever having married again. But I was satisfied. At least I knew that the reasons for my adoption were deeper than simply 'lack of accommodation'.

By the time I got home – I was still staying with my adoptive mother – I was totally overwhelmed by it all. There'd been so much going on, I felt relieved to be away from it. I still didn't tell my adoptive mother anything about my reunion. I didn't feel guilt about not telling her. Quite the reverse: I thought I was doing her a favour by not letting her know.

I was now keen to meet my half-siblings. The next weekend, I rang Hazel, and although the conversation with her was still strained, she invited me up to London.

When I arrived, she sat me down and basically 'interviewed' me, as if she was trying to work out whether I was worth knowing and whether I was going to be a problem. I hadn't known what to expect and it was all a bit strange: very different from meeting Maggie. My sister Alix also arrived, followed by my other sister, Georgie, who had driven from Devon especially. We all sat down and had dinner and things got easier. However, they still spent most of the time quizzing me about what I did, my lifestyle and where I was from. It was as if they were all ganging up together to find out about me, their long-lost half-brother. There was only one of me – so it was more difficult for me than it was for them.

It also became clear that there was a rift in the family, mainly between Maggie and Georgie. Apparently, Georgie had traced my half-brother – the one who was adopted – and hadn't told Maggie at first. The brother had then gone to live near Georgie and she'd even set him up in business. Since then though, he had refused to contact Maggie at all. Maggie was terribly hurt and had stopped speaking to Georgie. The rest of the family had taken sides.

Soon afterwards, I met Julia, my eldest half-sister. She was bad news. She lived in London as well, and I drove up to meet her. Once there, I was ushered into the sitting room and asked to sit at the table. After quizzing me, she started to tell me her life story and how she'd been terribly treated by everyone, including Maggie. That didn't go down very well with me at all. As far as I was concerned, even though she'd been put in children's homes, Maggie had always stayed in contact with her. I was the only one of all the siblings whom nobody had ever tried to contact or keep. I felt resentful.

It became clear that Julia had a huge chip on her shoulder. She told me we couldn't talk for long because her son would be coming in, as if I had to be kept a secret. Halfway through, Alix telephoned and they were obviously talking about me. I realised that my other sisters had acted as a scouting party to see whether I was 'OK' enough to meet Julia.

The real problem started when I began to probe about the family rifts: not only about Georgie and Maggie, but about other arguments as well. Julia's shutters went down immediately. That was it. She was really aggressive and asked me to go. I was shocked, but there was nothing to do but comply. It was all extremely uncomfortable. I'd only been there for half an hour and had been effectively kicked out.

All this happened about three years ago. Since then, I've been up to see Maggie in Scotland again, with my eldest son, Tristan. Last Christmas, Maggie stayed with Tina in London, and I went up for Boxing Day, which was very nice. Now we contact each other by 'phone every couple of months or so. We still get on well, but we're not exactly close. There's a slight distance between us: she occasionally stays with my sisters in London, yet, while she's there, she never seems to make any attempt to contact me.

I'm not really in touch with my sisters. I used to send my nieces and nephews birthday cards and presents, but I stopped when it became clear that they weren't doing the same for my children. The truth is that they're not really my family. They certainly haven't extended me a warm family welcome. Basically, we're related by blood, but they're total strangers. There's no brother–sister bond whatsoever.

I am happy that I've traced them all though. I'm very protective towards Maggie, and if she had a problem, I'd help her out. If my sisters ever needed anything that I could give, then I would give. We're not close, but it's nice to know the answers to the questions I used to have. It has cauterised the wound of rejection a little.

I think it's very important for adoptees to meet their natural parents. Whatever the outcome, it makes you feel 'whole' and soothes the hurt of the past. You need to know the truth, find out the reasons why and put it behind you. It's also a great thing for the natural mother. The relief for her, when her child comes back and says 'Don't feel guilty. I don't blame you,' must be like a having a huge weight lifted from her shoulders.

I still feel a deep resentment towards my adoptive family and the way I was treated by them. I'm still there for my adoptive mother: she's now quite old and I visit her regularly and look after her. But when she dies, I'm determined that I will change my surname, and my sons' names – probably back to my birth father's name. It will show that I still stand alone.

Sue

I was brought up by a modest, ordinary little family in a small seaside town in Dorset. My adoptive mother had been told she couldn't have any children, so in late 1950 she and her husband adopted me. I grew up as an only child. I always knew I was adopted, but I didn't really know what it meant. I was told I was 'special' and 'chosen', and when I was nine or ten, I remember sitting and watching a TV programme on the subject. My parents allowed me to stay up and watch, even though it was on late. As I did, the penny slowly dropped. I suddenly realised the difference between a 'real' mum and an adopted mum. Over the next weeks, I got some stick at school. Other children kept taunting me about how they'd got a 'real' mum and I hadn't. I suppose their parents had been talking and they'd somehow picked up on things.

My parents were very much of the old school: real disciplinarians. I felt quite close to my mum but my dad was a distant figure. I was in awe of him as he was the one who dished out any punishment. They didn't really talk much about anything, so the subject of my adoption never came up. There were a couple of major arguments, when I remember shouting that they weren't my real parents anyway, but that was it. I was scared of upsetting the apple cart by broaching the subject.

I also remember strange little things, which I suppose all adopted children experience. For instance, when I went to social occasions with my parents, I'd sometimes be told how much I looked like them. That used to hurt. But, generally, because of the way my parents were, I knew I had to just get on with things.

Now I look back and I can see how it's affected me over the years. It wasn't a normal upbringing and it set the pattern for the rest of my life. Unfortunately, I have a rather depressive personality and my life has turned out to be one long guessing game. I've also always had a strong fear of losing my friends. I have no problem getting on with people, but I was, and am, quite possessive. I suppose I'm scared of being rejected again. I've also always been quite jealous of people with brothers and sisters. Not truly jealous, but envious that they have other siblings who are always there for them.

When I was thirteen, I started to rebel slightly. My parents used to go out every Sunday afternoon and I started to refuse to go with them. One day, they went off and I went sneaking through the house. I found my adoption documents, which told me my birth mother's name, Diana; and my original name – Frances. I stole them and locked them in a drawer in my bedroom, but they disappeared a few days later. My mum had obviously taken them back. It was a huge shock, discovering my real name. It was as if the document was about a completely different person; it took me ages to absorb. The nice thing about it was that I preferred the name Frances to Susan. My parents never asked me why I'd removed the document and, as was typical, the subject was never raised.

I left school at fifteen and started work at the Post Office. I was having problems at home and revelling in my new-found freedom from school and my dad. I discovered soon afterwards that I was pregnant and I panicked. I didn't tell any of my friends, least of all my parents. But I went to the doctor and he insisted that I tell Mum and Dad. I was terrified.

I told Mum and she was devastated. It was a nightmare, especially when she told Dad. They got together with the doctor and I was told that I had to have an abortion. I became hysterical. They had made the decision for me and I hadn't been consulted. I was extremely angry and their behaviour made me even more determined to keep the baby. So I went ahead. My baby daughter, Emma, was born when I was seventeen and I kept her.

I took Emma back home to my parents. I desperately wanted to give up work to look after her, but they wouldn't allow it. I was told that Mum would care for the baby while I was out at work. The arrangement only lasted around three months because I couldn't bear the thought of someone else pushing my baby around in a pushchair, to the shops, out to the park. It was me who should be doing that. I felt that my rights as a parent were being taken away. The upshot of it all was that I had a major row with my parents, and I left home, leaving Emma with them. Being apart from her was awful.

The rescue came when my boyfriend, Emma's father, turned up again, and all three of us moved into a flat of our own. (I later married him and we had four more children.) A few months later, when I was eighteen, my boyfriend suggested that I ask my mother if I had any German or Scandinavian blood in me – because I was so blonde. I was terrified about asking her anything about my history, but this time I plucked up enough courage. I went over to see her, my heart beating, and asked her outright whether I was foreign. She replied, 'No, no, no, my girl, you're British to the core.'

I grabbed the opportunity to ask her more. She told me that all she knew was that my birth father had been a diamond merchant and that my birth mother was a private secretary – details which she had been told. I later found out that none of them were true and since then, I've had a major problem with lies and deceit. I hate all forms of them.

Time passed and I didn't do anything more until I was twenty-three or so. I contacted the mother-and-baby home where I knew I'd been born and a lady who'd run the nursery where I was looked after before my adoption. I telephoned her and told her I was adopted and trying to find my real parents. She asked what my original name had been and I told her. She immediately said, 'You were one of my babies, dear. I remember you.' She invited me to go and see her the next week. I did, and told her my story. She said she could remember me well and where my cot had been in the nursery. She also told me that my adoptive mum and dad had been interested in two babies – me and another baby girl. The other baby had something wrong with her leg, so they'd chosen me. We then talked about my getting hold of my birth certificate, although that wasn't legal at the time. She told me to leave it with her. A few days later, I went to the local Registry Office and paid £2.50 for it.

I remember holding the certificate in my hands for ages. I couldn't leave the building, I just stood in a corridor holding it. It had an address on it: where my mother had stayed during her pregnancy. I was incredibly elated and in a state of total disbelief. I rushed to the address straight away, but of course, no one there could remember anything.

Over the next few months, I made several trips to St Catherine's House and found my birth mother's birth certificate. I also searched for my father's – as my adoption documents had given me a name – but could find no trace of him. However, I had a lead to go on: my mother's certificate had an address in Surrey on it. I immediately wrote a letter to the address enquiring about her, but the person living there didn't know anything. I also wrote to neighbours of the address, but again, drew a blank. I started writing to any organisation which might have had connections with my mother, but I got nowhere.

I continued to look for her. However, there were times when I had to stop for a few months, because it was taking over my life. I had four children to look after, and my search was not only getting very expensive, but very time-consuming.

By the time I was thirty-one, I'd almost given up. However, one day, I was on a train, and I met a man who worked for United Artists. He said he was a friend of Ed Stewart's, the Radio 2 DJ. I don't know why, but I got talking to him and told him my story. He said that Ed Stewart did a spot on his show called 'Where are you now?' and he offered to arrange a request on my behalf. I thought about the offer for a few days and then decided to go ahead. It seemed to be my last chance.

The day of the broadcast came and the request went out on air. I didn't hear it all, because a weird thing happened. I was sitting in the sitting room with the radio on when there was a knock on the door. It was my dad, who had never, ever turned up at the house before without ringing to arrange it. I hadn't told him about my search, so I rushed back into the sitting room and snapped the radio off – just as my address was being announced. Luckily, he didn't 'click' what was going on.

I received a letter from my mother the very next day.

My dear Frances,
Please ring the above number. I'm desperate to have a chat with you.
I wanted to rush over, but I thought you'd prefer to talk first.
Love, Mummy

She'd responded immediately! I was ecstatic. I called her the same day. It was terribly nerve-racking. I was terrified as I dialled the number. My first thought was that I couldn't tell her I lived in a council house and had four children. I had in my mind the fact that my father was a diamond merchant, and my mother's voice sounded very posh. I thought she would be disappointed at the way I'd turned out.

In the end, Diana and I spoke for over an hour. She didn't sound like me at all – her voice was very soft, unlike mine. She was very easy to talk to, but I didn't feel a rapport. She felt like a stranger, which she effectively was. But the conversation was great, there was so much to catch up on, and I could have talked all day. She told me I had two half-sisters. We covered everything in the end, her life and mine.

I want to say here that ever since childhood, I'd always had this gut feeling that I would meet my birth mother in Torquay. She'd lived there for a time, something which I'd discovered in my searching, so maybe that was what triggered my 'instinct' off. But during our 'phone call, we arranged to meet at my house, about an hour away from Torquay. She would drive down with my two sisters and we could talk in private.

Once we'd set the day, I went mad with the preparations. I bought everything – smoked salmon, strawberries, the whole works. I was determined she wouldn't think I was 'below' her.

It came to the day and time itself and Diana didn't arrive. Time went on and on and still she didn't turn up. I was pacing up and down. It was agony. Finally, the 'phone rang. She told me that they'd had a car accident on the way down – it wasn't serious – and asked me if I could get to Torquay, where we could all meet up at her mother's house. It was so weird – I'd always known we'd meet in Torquay – and my 'premonition' had come true!

Nothing, nothing, would have stopped me getting there. I agreed instantly and rushed to get a train. During the journey, my stomach began churning beyond belief. This was it. I was really going into the unknown and it was the strangest, strangest feeling. I kept wondering whether she'd be there when I arrived and what she would be like. It was sheer nerves, sheer excitement.

Somehow, I got to the right address on time and knocked on the door. Diana's mother – my grandmother! – a tiny, petite old lady, answered and put her arms around me immediately. 'Oh Frances,' she said, 'There hasn't been a day that's passed when I haven't thought about you.' She told me that Diana hadn't arrived yet, so I had even more waiting to do at my grandmother's house.

Finally, Diana turned up. I can't tell you: my heart was almost beating out of my chest. I stayed in the sitting room and my grandmother let her in. Then she walked into the room. My heart stopped. She had bleached blonde hair and bright red nails. She immediately held her arms out to me. 'Oh my darling!' she cried, 'I've waited so long for this day! I've let you go once and I'm never going to let you go again.' I didn't particularly like the last bit, it was so sweeping, but we hugged and hugged.

My two sisters, Sacha and Laura, who were in their mid-teens, also arrived and we all sat down and talked and talked. Each of their reactions had been different. Sacha, the elder, was very intrigued and excited to meet me. Laura, however, was a little bit hostile towards me. When Diana had first come clean and told her about me, she had, apparently, been disgusted that her mother had got pregnant outside of marriage. I didn't notice any similarities between me and the two girls.

I ended up staying until about nine o'clock that evening. I asked Diana about my father and she was quite open about him. He had been an antiques dealer in Torquay and his name was Roger. He had been married when she got pregnant; but after I'd been adopted, they had continued to see each other for eighteen years. I didn't particularly like hearing that, as I felt that perhaps she could have kept me after all. After that, however, Diana had married a man who was much younger than her, by whom she'd had Sacha and Laura. He had died when he was just thirty-six, just two months before our reunion.

Not long after our first meeting, I went to stay with Diana and my sisters for a week. It was an absolutely lovely time. Diana and I were very relaxed together, like old friends, and we talked all week. It was all very successful. We met again when Diana came to stay with me at my house for a few days. Again, everything went well. From then on, we started to meet up and stay with each other quite regularly, without a hitch.

About six weeks after my first meeting with Diana, I began to feel very guilty about my dad. (My adoptive mother had died ten years earlier.) I began to lose weight and was torturing myself about the fact that I hadn't told him about the situation. I can't bear hiding the truth in any way, so I knew I had to tell him. It was eating me up. I plucked up courage one day and his reaction was wonderful. He told me he was really happy for me as I'd already lost Mum and I needed to get to know Diana. A huge burden was instantly lifted from my shoulders. I was so relieved.

Later on, I gave Dad the choice to meet Diana if he wanted to. He decided that he would, and he came over one day during one of her stays with me. I remember it quite well. I felt awful for him while he was here. Diana has a very strong personality and was always flush with money and constantly flitting off on holidays and things. I remember looking at Dad while Diana was talking and thinking, 'Actually, you're the one who's always been there for me.' I suddenly realised that he'd been the strong one, the person I'd always been able to rely on. He was smashing towards Diana, but I felt very sad for him that day.

Between 1983 and 1991, I continued to meet Diana quite frequently. Things were going smoothly. My children had accepted her as their 'Nan', and it seemed that nothing could go wrong. In 1991, my eldest daughter, Emma, who was twenty-three by now, was diagnosed as having cancer. Everyone knew how serious her illness was, including Diana. It was a nightmare, and as a family, we were making endless visits to the Royal Marsden Hospital in London. During our early visits, I found out from Diana that her brother, my uncle, had died, leaving her quite a substantial sum of money.

I accepted the situation and thought nothing more about it. At some stage, I told Emma the news. She has a very fiery and outspoken streak in her, and not long after, she told me she'd written to Diana and told her what she thought of her. Apparently, she'd called her despicable for telling us her good news yet not offering us any financial help. From what she told me, she'd really let rip. Even though I knew she was in a highly emotional state due to her illness – it was very serious at that point and her doctors had told us to expect the worst – I still couldn't believe she had done it. I was very angry that she'd interfered, but there was nothing I could do.

A few days passed and there was silence from Diana. However, about a week later, the 'phone rang. It was her. 'Hello, darling,' she said. 'Did you know Emma had written to me?' I replied that Emma had told me. 'Let me read you the letter,' she went on. I told her there was no need to, as Emma had already told me what was written in it.

Diana ignored me and started to run Emma down. I sat and listened as she launched into a tirade. As I sat there, I began to wonder how she could continue pulling Emma apart when she knew how seriously ill she was. However, I kept quiet and continued to listen. By the time Diana had finished, I was boiling with anger, but I still hadn't said anything. She eventually stopped. I just said 'OK, then. Goodbye.' That was the last time I ever spoke to her.

I knew the moment I put the 'phone down that I wouldn't contact her again. If I have a fall out, that's it. I'm very stubborn. So I haven't called her and she hasn't contacted me since. I don't think she'll try to do so in the future either.

I'm not heartbroken about it. At the end of the day, I feel that it doesn't matter how bad your children are, you should still give them unconditional love. I had to stand up for Emma. I understand that Diana was upset by the letter, but her reaction was out of order considering the situation. I was also aware that although I would never have asked her for money, the fact was that she hadn't offered anything at all. I remember thinking, 'Yes, well, perhaps I'm not that struck on you after all.' The irony is that I think Diana and Emma are very much alike, and that's why there was a confrontation.

I'm not really bothered about keeping in contact with Sacha or Laura either. If one of them were to ring and say they were in my area and needed somewhere to stay, then they would be more than welcome. The only person I would love to contact now is my birth father. I'd like to find out his side of the story.

Despite the outcome, I'm pleased I found Diana. Had Emma not written the letter, I would still be in contact with her, but these things happen. I saw another side of her which I didn't like. Emma is now clear of her illness, and she's well. It's funny how things turn out.

How does my life feel now? I still feel 'adopted'. I don't have trouble forming relationships with people, but I have problems maintaining them. I think that's connected to my adoption.

My fear of deceit and lies stems from the misinformation on my original adoption documents. I hate the idea of people not telling me the truth. I have to have answers. I have to have the truth. I don't trust anyone, ever. I know that's sad, but that's the way I am. Depression haunts me, and my daughters always tell me it's because I'm adopted.

Jude

Behind the smiling face
There lies the deepest wound

Behind closed doors
It smiles no more
But bleeds

The blood has no colour
They are my tears
That will be washed away
And leave no trace
No blemish on the smiling face.

Jude 1982

For twenty-nine years, I harboured the wound. From time to time, it opened and bled; not very often though. The wound was the great big question mark hanging over me, the great unknown about my origins. Where did I come from? From whom did I come? Why was I given up for adoption, and what did 'she' look like? Interestingly, I gave little thought to my father. I had no history, no roots. I felt as if I could have fallen from the sky.

I had no delusions of grandeur. I never once fantasised that my natural mother came from high places. I gravitated to the strong possibility that I was a product of some poor woman who had been raped or maybe the end result of a prostitute and her client. I had the impression that my mother was feeble, weak and rather seedy – from the poor, lower classes I suspected – frail, and with greasy, unwashed hair.

This image of my birth mother probably came, albeit unintentionally, from my adoptive parents. They were terribly strict and religious, and regarded sex outside marriage as an occupation of the wayward. Ironically, the wayward was ultimately their salvation!

My parents were 'good sorts', middle class and well-meaning, but because the subtext was 'nice girls don't do that sort of thing', I subconsciously transferred the poorer aspect of my birth mother's image to myself. I became what I had come from: not seeing things through for fear that I was destined to fail anyway. After all, I wasn't really 'of' my very academic parents with their high expectations.

I also felt very unattractive and couldn't understand how I managed to be one of the most popular girls with the boys (a few girls also!) in my school, college, workplace and in general. Could it have been that I was naturally meant to be and act this way, that my waywardness was programmed before birth and contained within my DNA?

I knew very little about my birth mother, except that she must have been very caring to give me up for adoption. She chose the name Sinead for me, which when I was adopted at three months, was changed to Jude by my parents. I also knew that my natural mother's name was Myra and the name of the infamous Myra Hindley used to flash through my brain. That really was a blight for me at around the age of twelve to thirteen. If only it had been plain Jane or Susan, but Myra! I couldn't possibly be the illegitimate daughter of the most despised and hated woman in the land, could I? On seeing a photograph of Myra Hindley's face, I used to imagine there were great likenesses to my face (of course, there wasn't the remotest similarity, but I was obsessed). I thought that her eyes were mine, her broad nose was mine, her cold glare was mine, and likewise, her lips. I began to believe that every bad thing I did or evil thought I possessed – my anger, outbursts of violence or aggression, and dislike of small children (I wanted to physically hurt them, damage them) – were inherited from her. Intellectually, I thought the whole notion absurd, ridiculous and highly improbable, but intuitively, I believed it with a real vehemence, fearful that someone, some day would discover my real identity. Of course, no one did.

Years later when I had seen some of the world; was older, wiser and married with three small boys, I decided the time was right to go in search of my roots. I now knew how painful and heartbreaking it would have been for Myra to give me away and I wanted to thank her for giving me life – for without her, I would not have my beautiful, darling sons. I am pleased I have them, but I had children for the wrong reasons. I wanted to have someone related biologically to me. Although I no longer need to know, I still revel in the fact that my youngest son looks very like me.

I was under no illusions. I had resigned myself to a poor outcome: that Myra might not want to see me or was married and had not told her husband or family. I didn't even know if she was alive! I anticipated the worst, probably for my own emotional protection. However, on obtaining my original birth certificate, it took me just six weeks of hard investigation before I was rewarded with my first direct contact. I got this by tracking down a property in which Myra's family had lived some years ago, and the neighbour, luckily for me, knew the whereabouts of one of her sisters.

I just stared at the 'phone number and marvelled that I had got this far. But it was still only the beginning. I had to make this 'phone call. My body crept with the cold fear of the unknown. The name Cait Beckett glared at me from above the number. A name at last! A number and a name – a contact! It was hard to believe I could soon be speaking to someone who was related to me. I felt drenched with nervous apprehension. So much rested on this call. Would she be abrupt and rude, brusque and guarded? Of course, I had to go undercover in case she knew nothing of my existence. I had to prepare myself mentally to cope with the news of Myra's death. Should that be the case, my journey could never end: there would be no arrival.

On my original birth certificate, I had discovered that at the time of my birth, Myra had been living in London and working at the American Embassy. Armed with this knowledge, which was the vital backdrop to my pretence, I picked up the 'phone, shaking and sweating profusely. With almost uncontrollable, sticky-fingered tremors, I dialled the number which was to take me across the water to Ireland. I was desperate to come away with an address or telephone number for Myra: the crucial passport to my past, my very own origin of species! My heart was pounding and I felt as if I would choke as I waited for an answer. I remember half-hoping that Cait would be out, but I knew that I'd only have to suffer the awful adrenaline rush again if she was. A softly spoken woman with a very attractive lilt in her voice answered.

'Hello?'

'Oh hello. Can I speak to Cait Beckett please?'

'Yes, speaking.' Was I home and dry? The next question was so important. My mouth was dry and I quivered all over.

'I wonder if you will be able to help me? I was a friend of

Myra's when she worked at the American Embassy and I would love to get in touch with her again.'

The answer came back, 'She lives in New Zealand now, has done for many years. She emigrated in 1958.' Gulp for air, at least she was alive! Before I asked for an address or telephone number, I hesitated. I still don't know what made me ask the next question; it was unplanned and seemed to come from nowhere.

'Do you know who I am?'

'Yes, yes I do.' I could hardly believe what I had just said, let alone her reply. How could she know me? I was dumbfounded and thought I was going to be sick. Her voice was kind and caring.

'Who do you think I am then?' I said.

'No, I'd rather you said something first.' This was going to be the biggest gamble of my life, everything rested on my next word. I gave little thought to it, the word sprang from my mouth instinctively.

'Sinead.' I just knew; she knew me already.

'Ah yes, yes, yes!' She sighed with relief and delight. I can't remember what happened next, except the tears of joy we both shared together. I couldn't believe what had just happened. She told me Myra would be absolutely delighted and that I would have ended years of sadness, misery, guilt, heartache and longing. I couldn't believe I was hearing it all. She explained that Myra had emigrated to New Zealand when I was two years old. She was so heartbroken, she had wanted a completely fresh start. Her secret dream was that one day her tiny baby would try and find her and make contact. I knew that very soon I would be doing just that.

After endless questions about Myra, the colour of her hair, her eyes, the size and shape of her mouth and nose, we said our goodbyes, both knowing that this was not goodbye, only the beginning.

Minutes later, I received a 'phone call from another of Myra's sisters, Muriel. She too was overjoyed and in tears of disbelief. She said that the whole family would be ecstatic. She told me that only last year, Myra had been in Ireland and that they had spent hours walking along the beach, with Myra suffering from depression because of me. She had been longing for me, she thought about me all the time. I still couldn't believe that someone I didn't know could have feelings of such love for me. I felt very wanted and very excited. I was on the precipice of a whole new world. All the nervous apprehension ebbed from me. Muriel gave me Myra's telephone number, the combination to the safe that had never been unlocked; bade me farewell and welcome at the same time, and promised to put some photographs of my new family in the post. I could hardly wait! I also learned that Myra was married to Scott, a New Zealander, and that they had a son (my half-brother!) called Bede, nine years my junior. They both knew about me, and Muriel insisted that they would be over the moon at the happy outcome.

Nervously, I picked up the 'phone and rang New Zealand. I knew that it would be fairly early in the morning there, but I was so eager I didn't really care.

'Hello?' a man answered.

'Hello, please may I speak to Myra?' I replied, trying to appear calm when really my stomach was not in its rightful place.

'She's not here right now. Who is calling?' I remember thinking: Help! Does this man really know about me? Am I going to throw a huge spanner in the works and ruin everything? Go for it, I thought – so I did.

'It's her daughter.'

'Her daughter? ... Wow! Well howdie, how are you?' His voice soared an octave and rang with the excitement of somebody who had just been given the news of a rather large lottery win.

'She's just flown down to Auckland. In fact, that distant rumble is probably her plane going overhead right now! I'm Scott, Myra's husband by the way. Now, this is unbelievable! Myra will be absolutely over the moon!' His voice rang with excitement. Confirmation for me that all would be well, finally laying to rest my doubts and reservations.

'I'll drive down to Auckland where she's at a conference, and tell her the good news and get her to 'phone you. It'll take a good few hours, so with the time differences it will be your morning and our evening ... wow! I can't believe that I'm not dreaming!'

'OK then, that would be great. My name is Jude by the way.'

'OK Jude, I'll get right along now and Myra will 'phone you as soon as possible.'

It was brilliant. I was so excited I was on another plane. The wait was almost unbearable. I was overwhelmed with a warm, girlish glow of sheer joy. I was wanted from Ireland all the way to New Zealand, and I hadn't had a clue! I didn't care what she looked like, I just knew everything would be fine.

My husband Robert was thrilled for me. I could tell that he admired the relentless and determined way that I had left no stone unturned, and it had paid off! To toast the wondrous occasion, he opened a bottle of champagne, and for the first time in my life, I couldn't touch a drop. I just felt overdosed, saturated in adrenalin, drenched in my own euphoria. I couldn't eat either. My whole body was stuffed with hyperactive butterflies and the knots in my stomach, which had strayed from its usual place again, tightened like a stranglehold. In fact, every organ of my body had changed position! I was engulfed in a myriad of emotions: of belief, disbelief, tension, relief, guilt (betrayal of my adoptive parents), justification, sadness and happiness. I was sad because I was so happy. There is often a very thin line between joy and pain and I felt the line melt, fuelled by the heat of my passion. Joy and pain had fused into one emotion.

I couldn't wait to speak to Myra, and could hardly believe that within a few hours – fourteen, if I remember correctly – I would actually be speaking to the mother who bore me: my real flesh-and-blood mother. I was beside myself with ambivalence, consumed with the unreality and reality of it all. Soon I, her daughter, was to grant her a twenty-nine-year-old wish; satisfy her biggest, burning desire and end her longing. It was almost sexual, the same painful yet joyous, exquisite feelings of lust and longing – and power – sure in the knowledge of positive reciprocation. Seduction, oh such sweet seduction! I can't remember how I got through the night. It was either sleepless or probably greatly aided by a few soporific Scotches.

The 'phone rang soon after the children had gone to school. I grabbed it with nervous eagerness, hoping that just this once, it would not be one of my girlfriends, but her, Myra!

'Hello, is that you, Jude?'

'Yes it is, is that Myra?'

'Yeah, oh Jude, I can't believe it! Scott drove down here specially to tell me the news. He told me someone from the UK had 'phoned, but he wouldn't say who it was straight away. He was so excited, so I wasn't worried that anyone was in danger. I went through every member of the family and my friends and he said, "No, it was your daughter." It just didn't register with me at first. I was so dumb struck he had to repeat it "Your daughter, Myra," over and over. I just sobbed and sobbed and sobbed into my Scotch!'

'Are you happy?'

'Am I happy? I just can't believe it. I've had a little time to recover, but it all seems too good to be true. Tell me, Jude, are you well?'

'Yes, I'm fine and you?'

'Good, really good. Tell me about yourself.'

'Well, you are the grandmother of three boys.'

'Am I really? That's wonderful, how old are they?'

'Tom's five, Harry is nearly four and Toby is two. Tell me, do you smoke?'

'I confess I do and I like a few drinks too!' she laughed knowingly.

'Do you? So do I.'

'I can't believe this.'

'Nor can I, it's beyond words.' Again, ten years have robbed me of the memory of all the details of our first conversation, but she promised to send me lots of photographs and I vowed to do the same. Hearing her voice was just wonderful, she sounded so warm and loving. I felt I had known her all my life and just as Aristophanes in Plato's Symposium tells of the search for our other twin in pursuit of becoming whole again, I felt I had found my twin. We just 'clicked' and I knew I was on the brink of a beautiful relationship with all the wondrous feelings of a passionate love affair.

I received some photos from Muriel the next day. Looking at Myra was like looking at myself, only her hair was darker than mine. God, how over the years I had longed to look like someone! I kept studying the photographs of her.

Over the next few days, the most welcome sight in my life was the postman arriving. I had a surge of excitement every time his van entered my courtyard. Within a few days I received a large parcel, full of photos of Myra from when she was about eighteen to the present day. She was truly beautiful in her youth and I could see that the threads of beauty remained intact. She looked like a combination of Elizabeth Taylor, a sultry Joan Collins and an animated Liza Minelli. She was dark, whereas I was fair, and she was generally bigger built than I was, but the similarities were stunning. I raided my own box of photos and found many, almost identical. This was too good to be true. If I looked at her and thought that she was beautiful, then maybe – just maybe – I was too!

When I read her first letter, I was in my element. I absorbed every word as if it were a love letter. I smelt the paper, wanting to consume her.

Dearest Jude,

I still cannot believe that this is actually real, that I have really spoken to my daughter and have your lovely letter and photographs too. It is just too, too wonderful and I keep thinking that at any moment I am going to awaken from this beautiful dream. Jude, thank you for wanting to find me, and for being such a wonderful, understanding daughter. I am so proud of you and love you so much it hurts.

I have wanted so much to try and trace you, Jude. However to be loyal to your adoptive parents, I was going to wait until you were thirty years old, as I thought by that time you would be old enough to accept the idea of knowing that your mother loved you very much and had never for one moment, forgotten you. As I told you on the 'phone, on your twenty-ninth birthday, I just felt I couldn't wait another year, and I was going to take steps to trace you.

Like you Jude, I too, had the dreadful fear that if I did find you, you would not want to know me. I also had mixed feelings in respect of your adoptive parents, as I did not want to betray or upset them in any way, as I have nothing but the greatest respect and admiration for them. I also feel a love for them for taking my baby daughter into their hearts and for being such wonderful parents to you. I feel now that I have been reunited with you, God has forgiven me.

Myra's second letter continued in the same vein.

I have to keep pinching myself to assure myself that the very beautiful young lady I am looking at in the photos is my darling daughter. Oh Jude, it was because of the love I had for you that I did what I did, at that time in my life. When I got permission at the 'Adoption House', it nearly broke my heart to leave you there. The Matron was so very kind, she let me feed you, and hold you; it was wonderful, and whilst I held you close to me, Jude, I told you then how much I loved you, and that I would always love you, even though I could not be with you. When the Matron told me I had to leave, I was very, very upset, especially when I asked her if I could visit you again and she told me 'no', as your adoptive parents were coming for you the very next day. I said a final goodbye to my baby, knowing I would never see you again.

How delightfully wrong she was! The next few months were spent writing copious reams to each other, telling all. I told her everything about me: the good, the bad and the ugly. I knew that whatever I had done in my past didn't matter, because for the first time in my life the love I received was unconditional, something I'd never felt before.

I was to meet her in May and week by week, the thrilling excitement grew more intense. With my adrenal glands working to full capacity, I lost a lot of weight and we were also blessed with an incredibly abundant, sunny spring. Consequently, I was sylph-like and tanned and looked wonderful. I wanted to look my best for her. It was like being in love.

I remember our last 'phone conversation before she was due to leave New Zealand. It was quite a revelation.

'The flight is so long, how will you combat it?'

'Oh, I'll read.'

I was prepared for her to come out with, say, Danielle Steele or Mills and Boon, anything chocolate-boxey. But, no.

'I like George Eliot, Jane Austen, that sort of thing. Balzac and Proust not really my bag.' Such enlightenment! My tastes might be nature as much as nurture.

I can't remember now when her plane was due in. What I can remember is being at the airport and suffering an overwhelming urge to go to the loo. It was as if I was gripped with a primeval fear: I'd run faster if I was lighter – survival! So I went to the loo and then joined Robert, in gorgeous anticipation, in the Arrivals lounge.

I saw her, she saw me: instant recognition. Although we had the photos of each other, photos are static. It was like love at first sight. We kissed, hugged, cuddled. I was consumed by such a powerful love, that we both shone in the effulgence of our shared exuberance, both mental and physical. Two bodies became one. Time and travellers left us and just as twenty-nine years before, we were one and the same. The journey home was filled with endless chatter, and poor, dear Robert, in his silence, was generous to a fault.

The next two weeks were sheer bliss: heaven on earth.

Endless kisses and hugs, admiration bursting from her to me. I was told how beautiful, how talented, how musical, how creative, how intelligent I was. This was utterly alien to me. Men had told me about my beauty before, but I had always suspected that it was advance payment for a ticket to a performance, in which they performed with me. The praise from Myra was endless and I blossomed daily.

I was to learn very little about my father from her, because little was known. He had been in the US Air Force and as soon as he found out Myra was pregnant, he confessed to having a fiancé in the States and, in that direction, made a hasty retreat, leaving Myra totally alone with a couple of supportive friends ... and me, probably at this time, the size of a pinhead.

The time came for her to return to Ireland to visit her family. She left, leaving me bereft. I was so devastated that she sent me an air ticket and I immediately flew to Dublin to be with her. I had such a welcome from the family, I felt I had come home. Meeting Cait, Muriel and the rest of the family was simply wonderful, I felt so at one with them all. It was like a completed jigsaw puzzle.

One of the best days of my life was walking with Myra, arms linked, around Dublin. No one else mattered, I was with the love of my life. I scarcely gave a thought to Robert and the boys. I became increasingly possessive, wanting her all to myself. I can recall one evening, when she was particularly tired and went to bed earlier than anyone else. We had, with her sister, my aunt, been sharing a bed, and that night, I took a blanket and slept elsewhere. I wanted her exclusively, I absolutely adored her.

After a wonderful week, I had to return to my family. I left Dublin and spent the next few days on the brink of suicide. A few days later, Myra rejoined us before leaving for Heathrow.

I can recall our goodbye afternoon. It was dreadful. I had found this wonderful love and all too soon it was leaving me. My heart heaved and ached with sorrow and I felt physically sick at having to say goodbye. We cradled each other and we were both disturbed by the painful parting that was all so imminent. Sadness shrouded me as I clung to her urgently and kissed her one last kiss goodbye.

I was so totally, utterly desperate when I drove away and left her. Many different combinations of suicide went through my mind. I wanted to be with her, but I had a young family, a husband and parents who would have been devastated had I relinquished and taken my own life.

You were the light
in my life.

Now you've gone.

You know, nothing survives
without light.

Jude 1985

I can't remember clearly – as I was enveloped in an oppressive, opaque, emotional fog – but I felt broken for days. As time passed and I busied myself in the clockwork, tick-tock monotony of domestic chores and the distraction of maternal duties, my emotional bones gradually seemed to repair. The painful psychological sling could finally be discarded. At last, I was mending. The prognosis looked much brighter.

Self-pity eventually ebbed from me and, like new blood, optimism started to filter through my veins. Perspective, like a loyal friend (who had always been there, but whom I hadn't seen) was coming back into my life. My senses pricked with lucidity and I could see that there were more than 11,000 miles between Myra and me. Although we had identical mannerisms, I had no history with her. My background was solid with my parents and my caring, loving grandparents. They were responsible for my wonderful moments of childhood nostalgia. It was from them that I got my social, emotional, cultural and political proclivities. Although my reunion had been terribly important to me, I began to realise that biological attachment is far less important than the secure social cradle that had carried and occasionally rocked me to where I am now.

Eleven years on, I still keep in touch with Myra, and she with me. She has since visited me twice and has written with more regularity. I occasionally 'phone her and it is always good to hear her voice. I hope to be able to visit her in New Zealand some day, but out of loyalty to my adoptive parents, will not do so while they are still alive. If, in the unnatural order of things, I die before them, then so be it.

To me, it is all now a *fait accompli* in a way. My reunion was mind-blasting and I now have the confidence, having read it, to put it back on the bookshelf, along with all the other books, where it belongs: an experience amongst experiences. I have a contentment now that I did not have before. I no longer sleep with that daunting question mark hanging over me. The great unknown is now known. The wound that lay behind the smiling face has healed.

As darkness falls
and hangs her velvet cloak
and sleep hangs heavy on my lids.

I think of morning!
Oh such sweet morning
and hope she brings you
gently to your day.

While unearthly hours
demand my rest
and silence loudly
calls me to my bed

I think of you,
alive and well
and in such knowledge
turn to face the stairs.

Jude 1985

Appendix

Useful Names and Addresses

Adoptees considering searching for their birth parents may find the following organisations helpful in their tracing. Many of the organisations listed can also provide emotional support, not only during the search itself, but also after any reunion. It is advisable to enclose a stamped addressed envelope when writing to any of the agencies featured.

There are many other post-adoption or after-adoption counselling centres throughout the UK. Their details can be obtained from your local Social Services department.

Adopted Children's Register
General Register Office (Adopted Section)
Smedley Hydro
Trafalgar Road
Southport
Merseyside PR8 2HH
Tel: 0151-471 4200

General Register for Scotland
New Register House
3 West Register Street
Edinburgh EH1 3YT
Tel: 0131-334 0380

National Organisation for Counselling Adoptees and Parents (NORCAP)
112 Church Road
Wheatley
Oxford OX33 1LO
Tel: 01865 875000

Scottish Adoption Association Limited
2 Commercial Street
Edinburgh EH6 6JA
Tel: 0131-553 5060

Post-adoption Centre
5 Torriano Mews
Torriano Avenue
Kentish Town
London NW5 2RZ
Tel: 0171-284 0555

After Adoption Wales
Unit 1
Cowbridge Court
58–62 Cowbridge Road West
Cardiff CF5 5BS
Tel: 01222 575318

British Agencies for Adoption and Fostering (BAAF)
Skyline House
200 Union Street
London SE1 OLX
Tel: 0171-593 2000

Parent-to-Parent Information on Adoption Services (PPIAS)
Lower Boddington
Nr Daventry
Northamptonshire NN11 6YB
Tel: 01327 260295